# *LOVE*
## IS A CHOICE

# *LOVE*
## IS A CHOICE

### 28 EXTRAORDINARY
### STORIES OF THE
### 5 LOVE LANGUAGES®
### IN ACTION

# Gary Chapman
## with JAMES STUART BELL

MOODY PUBLISHERS
CHICAGO

Edited by Avrie Roberts
Interior design: Brandi Davis
Cover design: Erik M. Peterson
Cover photo of holding hands by aranprime, courtesy of Unsplash.
Cover photo of wedding couple by Gabriela Monalisa, courtesy of Unsplash.
Cover photo of three guys laughing by Jed Villejo, courtesy of Unsplash.
Cover photo of smiling grandparents by Joe Hepburn, courtesy of Unsplash.
Cover photo of mother and son by Nathan Anderson, courtesy of Unsplash.
Cover photo of dad and child by Nathan Dumlao, courtesy of Unsplash.
Cover photo of three women by Priscilla Du Preez, courtesy of Unsplash.
Cover photo of people holding tablet by Surface, courtesy of Unsplash.

Library of Congress Cataloging-in-Publication Data

Names: Chapman, Gary D., 1938- author. | Bell, James S., author.
Title: Love is a choice : 28 extraordinary stories of the 5 love languages
   in action / Gary Chapman ; with James S. Bell Jr.
Other titles: Love is a verb
Description: Chicago : Moody Publishers, 2023. | "Originally published
   under the title Love Is a Verb by Bethany House Publishers, a division
   of Baker Publishing Group, Grand Rapids, Michigan 49516, U.S.A."--T.p.
   verso. | Summary: "Real life, encouraging stories embodying the bold,
   brave, and beautiful choice to love. If you're feeling weary or burdened
   by the call to love, you'll find strength and hope in the pages of this
   book. Each story is coupled with 5 Love Languages insights and
   application points"-- Provided by publisher.
Identifiers: LCCN 2022036857 (print) | LCCN 2022036858 (ebook) | ISBN
   9780802429025 (paperback) | ISBN 9780802473998 (ebk)
Subjects: LCSH: Love. | Love--Religious aspects--Christianity. |
   Interpersonal relations.
Classification: LCC BF575.L8 C44 2023  (print) | LCC BF575.L8  (ebook) |
   DDC 152.4/1--dc23/eng/20221004
LC record available at https://lccn.loc.gov/2022036857
LC ebook record available at https://lccn.loc.gov/2022036858

Originally delivered by fleets of horse-drawn wagons, the affordable paperbacks from D. L. Moody's publishing house resourced the church and served everyday people. Now, after more than 125 years of publishing and ministry, Moody Publishers' mission remains the same—even if our delivery systems have changed a bit. For more information on other books (and resources) created from a biblical perspective, go to www.moodypublishers.com or write to:

Moody Publishers
820 N. LaSalle Boulevard
Chicago, IL 60610

1 3 5 7 9 10 8 6 4 2

*Printed in the United States of America*

Dedicated to
*Derek and Amy Chapman,*
whose lifestyle demonstrates
that "love is a choice."

# Contents

# Acknowledgments

I am indebted to those individuals who shared their stories of love with me. This book would not have been possible without their contributions. I am extremely grateful to Jim Bell, who encouraged this project from the beginning and played the major role in collecting the stories. I hope that both he and the contributors will be rewarded by knowing that their work has helped others discover that love is a choice. I'm also grateful to others on the editorial and marketing side who played a role.

On the personal side, I have been greatly blessed with a son, Derek, and a daughter-in-law, Amy, who have for all of their married lives provided a model of what it means to love. Beginning with their wedding in Prague and continuing with their ministry in Antwerp, and now in Austin, Texas, they have been involved daily in giving their lives away to others. I dream of a day when their example will be multiplied, and to that end I have dedicated this book to them.

**GARY D. CHAPMAN**
Winston-Salem, North Carolina

# Introduction

*GARY CHAPMAN*

L ove makes the world go 'round."
  "All you need is love."
"Love can make you crazy . . ."

As long as any of us can remember, poems, songs, films, and orators have tried to adequately describe and express love. Movies and TV programs focus on the pursuit of love and personal fulfillment. Advertisements use this strong sentiment to sell us products. Our culture often seems to have a love-tracked mind.

Whether it's in marriage, family, or friendships, it's no wonder that love is such a draw and places so high on the priority list in our lives. After all, the wisest book I've ever read, the Bible, tells us that God Himself is love.

Few emotions in life equal the exciting adrenaline rush of a newfound romance or the sweet companionship of a friend or the faithful support of a family member. No wonder we seek love above so many other positive experiences. The normal, everyday challenges are so much easier to survive when we know we have people who are always there when we need them and support us unconditionally.

Because every love relationship involves fallible humans, challenges abound. Unlike the personal connections portrayed on the big and small screens, the real issues between people usually can't be resolved within thirty minutes, or even a few episodes. Sometimes circumstances and people make it almost impossible to love successfully.

The euphoria subsides after marriage, and the romantic feelings might fly out the window. We have a sharp disagreement and find ourselves being antagonistic instead of supportive.

Sometimes communication quandaries occur. At other times, we may cling to unrealistic expectations. And at other times, frankly, we may not actually know how love factors into the equation. And when the going gets tough, some people just get going . . . leaving a trail of wounded hearts behind.

As a pastor and counselor, I've seen it over and over again. A spouse gets bored with marriage and gives in to the temptation to see if the grass really is greener in another person's yard. Parents and children emotionally excommunicate each other over a misunderstanding. Someone sits alone at church or stays home because he or she has lost a friend and is afraid to become vulnerable and reach out again.

I've seen too many people give up on love too fast. Walking away from relationships doesn't provide the hoped-for relief, bring solutions, or simplify life. Rather, it piles on more problems through the lingering resentment and finger-pointing.

So, what are the answers to the challenges love brings? For starters, to last for the long haul and through the stresses and complexities of life, love has to be more than something we feel. It has to be something we do. We have to demonstrate it concretely in our marriage, our family, among our friends and acquaintances, and, yes, even among our enemies.

And that's what this book is about. In the following pages, you'll see examples of people just like you—like *all* of us—who learned to take the obstacles, the "lemons" they face in life, and turn them into satisfying, emotional thirst-quenching nectar. These are the success stories that make you want to go out and try harder.

You'll read about:

- Doris, who kept her hands busy furiously knitting when she almost felt like using them to strangle the husband she truly couldn't stand any longer.
- Faith, who had to learn how to cope when a stranger's mind inhabited her loved one's body.
- Laquita, who finally fell in love with her husband after forty years.
- Steven, who gave a cup of hot coffee to warm the love circulation in his heart; and Tamara, who learned that she had the power to enhance a less fortunate person's world.
- Rebecca, whose father was incapable of showing emotion.
- Midge, the woman who expected chocolate and ended up with a bitter taste in her mouth.
- Pamela, who ended up finding the treasure of her heart beneath the lid of a small silver box.

All of these people, and more, share their tales of learning to live out love through tragedy and triumph. Their experiences are more mesmerizing than any contrived Hollywood chronicles could be. You'll be able to connect with their narratives and relate to their angst and achievements.

And after each story, I've highlighted a key element that can help you become unbeatable in your quest for strong, stable re-lationships, as well as some practical love language observations and suggestions for you to make love a choice. Through these pages, I'll give you practical pointers these people used that you can also put into action. These stories will inspire you to build, rekindle, and experience the kind of love and friendship that endures after the warm fuzzy feelings have faded.

So, do you want to enjoy the best relationships possible? Then get to work. Love isn't wrapped up in a pronoun—in "he," "she," or "them." It's not about who other people are or how they treat us or what they do to make us value them. It begins with you, and it's not primarily about what you say or feel. Instead, love is an action word. *Love is a choice!*

# Loving Lavishly

*TAMARA VERMEER*

Tony walked into our office one day where my husband, Tim, counsels disabled veterans. His brilliant smile lit up his face. He was no taller than my fourteen-year-old—bald, rail thin, and in his late forties. He was so charming, the kind of charm that I'm sure his mother couldn't resist even if he'd been bad. He had this laugh, a half giggle that came so easily I almost laughed too—I couldn't help it. I met him only briefly, but he left an imprint on my heart that at first I didn't even realize was there.

Later that week Tim asked me, "Do you remember Tony?"

"Sure," I said, as I sorted mail.

"Let me tell you a little more about him. He has HIV, is a Katrina refugee, was relocated here to Denver, and from what I can tell he's completely alone. He's been homeless but recently found subsidized housing. However, he's pretty sick, his apartment is basically empty, and he's sleeping on the floor. He doesn't even have a bed."

*He doesn't even have a bed—no bed, and he's sick.* The words echoed through my mind. *No bed, no bed.* I pictured little Tony curled up on the floor. I've heard of desperate situations like this before, like we all do, and it always grips my heart and I feel terrible. But this time it was like someone shook me and yelled, "He doesn't have a bed! Look at all you have!"

Our family has always enjoyed helping the less fortunate—Christmas gifts to people in hardship, bringing meals to families with someone in the hospital, money to a child in Africa. But those were "safe" ways to help, and then we'd go home; our lives had never intertwined with them.

My stomach tilted and I felt a little shaky. I had to get him a bed. I don't know why this time I had to act, but God knew. And it had to be a new bed! For some reason, I wanted to love him *lavishly*. But even as I felt so driven to help him, I wondered what I was getting myself into. I'd never done anything like this before.

We delivered his bed and brand-new bedding that my girls and I had picked out. I was pretty nervous. He sat on his new bed, smoothed out the covers, and smiled. Then emotion overcame him and he sobbed. Coughs wracked his thin body.

"Thank you. Thank you so much—I don't know what to say. I . . . I . . ." His words drowned in the tears. This bed seemed to be a light in a very dark, deep pit. He looked at us with something like grateful confusion. I don't know how else to describe it. He didn't know us at all.

"Tony, dear! What's goin' on in here?" Juanita, his grandmotherly neighbor from across the hall, walked in. "I'm sure not lookin' right to meet new folks, but I wanted to see what's goin' on!"

She saw his bed and looked at Tony, shook her graying head, and said, "Honey, I told you God would take care of you. He heard you; yes, He did."

Our friends and family jumped right in—new pots and pans, dishes, towels, microwave, money—you name it! And to top it off, my sister Laurie bought him all-new furniture—not everyone's throwaways, but brand-new, matching furniture with a matching rug.

"Laurie," I said, "I'm kind of nervous about your spending this much money. We don't really know him, and he could sell it or someone could steal it or . . ."

"I want to do this, and whatever happens, happens," she said with a smile. Lavish love.

I called one day to check on him. He always had a positive twist on everything. "Well, I'm pretty good, pretty good today. Did you know tomorrow is my birthday?"

"Tony, let's have a birthday party!" My family came, along with my parents and even my daughter's friend. We wrapped the remaining things people had given in colorful bags and brought a cake. He sat on the couch, sandwiched between my parents, and the tears flowed. "I've never had a party like this before! I'm one of fourteen kids, you know."

I had no idea. Where was his family? Little slices of his life started to tumble out.

As we drove home, my daughter's friend smiled as she looked out the window and said, "That was the best day ever." When I returned later to take him some food, he had stapled all the gift bags onto his wall.

Tony started to get sicker. He had a lot of chest pain and difficulty breathing. I called to check on him one Monday morning. "I've been in the hospital three times this weekend, Tamara. I had terrible chest pain."

"Oh, Tony!" I felt terrible. "How did you get there?"

"I took the bus, but I had to walk a mile to the bus stop. They said they couldn't find anything so they sent me home, but I wasn't any better so I went back two more times."

They never even helped him get home! I was livid. In my world I had family to take me, and a car, and they never would have sent me home like that. In his world he was alone, and they didn't care.

I realized he needed a medical advocate, so Tim and I decided to step in. Perhaps because of his history, perhaps because he was alone, he continued to be treated as if he were not worth the medical professionals' respect or effort. He was hospitalized over and over, and I can't tell you how many times I roared to the hospital when I heard how he was treated. The nurses would ask, "And who are you?"

I'd act offended and say, "Well, his big sister, of course! Can't you see the resemblance?" He's black and 5'6" and I'm white and 5'10".

Tony got worse. I sat with him as he waited to see an oncologist one day. Tony was scared. He turned to me and said, "Why are you doing this? You don't really know me and the things I've done."

I smiled and said, "Well, you don't really know me and the things *I've* done."

"No, really," he urged.

"I think I just happened to be listening to God, Tony. He knew you needed someone to walk beside you right now and just love you."

Tony had lung cancer. We didn't know how much time he had left, and my sister felt an urgency to reunite him with his family. We urged him to call his mom. She lived in Mississippi.

"Oh, I don't want to worry her. She's almost eighty," he said. But wistfulness edged his voice. That was the first we'd heard of his mother, Lucille.

My parents started to visit him at his apartment and at the hospital. He called them momma and papa, and he often cried when he talked to them on the phone. I think he missed his own momma so much.

One night around eight o'clock he called from the hospital. "The doctor is here and . . ." His voice cracked and my throat constricted as he said, "It's not so good, big sister."

He tried to laugh, but it turned to sobs. The doctor took the phone and told me, without emotion, that Tony had stage-four lung cancer, and maybe six weeks to four months to live. I was so angry I was shaking. I had asked the people at the hospital to call me so I could be with him when they gave him the prognosis. To be told such news all alone is even more devastating.

We rushed to the hospital. To my surprise, Tony smiled, held my hands, and this time the tables were turned—he comforted me! I cried and cried.

"I know you think that doctor is mean, but I needed to hear the truth, and no one would tell me," he said.

I realized then how much I really loved Tony.

Tony told me later that after he'd gotten that news he left his room, walked downstairs, and had planned to walk out the door of the hospital and disappear for good. "I went back upstairs because I told you I'd be here and I didn't want to let you down. If it wasn't for you guys, I wouldn't be here now."

He called the next day and sang on my answering machine. And he laughed that laugh that made me laugh and then made me cry. "I used to sing with the Mississippi Mass Choir," he told me. Another slice of his life came out.

We continued to press him to call his family. He finally called his sister Cynthia. My sister, with her generous, lavish heart, offered to fly Cynthia to Denver *and* rent her a car. Cynthia had no idea he was so sick. "I don't understand why he didn't call us sooner! I would have come before this."

He had distanced himself from his family for reasons they still don't understand. It was obvious they loved him. But life had hurt him deeply somehow.

Cynthia came out, and one night at his apartment she shared her heart. "You know, I've had some back problems and I haven't been able to work, but I've felt like there must be something I should be doing. 'Lord,' I prayed, 'what is my purpose? What do you want me to do?' Well, this is the answer. I'm supposed to take Tony home and take care of him."

The Veterans Administration paid for Tony's flight, and my sister paid for Cynthia's flight. When Tony went home, I knew I would never see him again.

His family flocked to see their lamb that had strayed. His brothers and sisters came from all over the country, and his daughters came—yes, he had two daughters and four grand-children! His story kept unfolding.

His mom never left his side. She called me one day and told me, "I had been praying for a miracle for my Tony, and you were that miracle." Tony died that May. He fell asleep and never woke up, but he died with his family around him. He wasn't alone anymore.

Tony's family included our family photo in his funeral pro-gram with the following words: "We could not have had a better family than you to take care of our beloved Tony. Saying thank you is not enough! You deserve more. May God bless you and keep you."

I took a chance to tip my heart and let some lavish love spill out, and look what happened: a very unexpected love story.

*Sometimes in life we take a chance on someone. That decision makes the stomach tilt and our hands a little shaky. We don't have to do it, no one will know if we don't, and our lives would continue the same as always. But when we start to love, not only as a tentative experiment but also lavishly, our lives are changed forever. When we love generously, we receive unforgettable rewards. And sometimes, that caring touches not only the other person but has a ripple effect, creating an "extended family" that becomes an experience of true community that we all long for.*

### THE 5 LOVE LANGUAGES IN ACTION

Tamara and her family spoke three of the love languages fluently—*gifts, acts of service*, and *quality time*—and they spoke them to a total stranger whom God put in their path. One cannot read this account without sensing the deep sense of joy and satisfaction that came from loving lavishly.

### LOVE IS A CHOICE

Would you pray that God would lead you to someone whom you could love by speaking one or more of the five love languages?

Remember Jesus said that at the last judgment He would say to those on His right hand: "'Come, you who are blessed by my Father; take your inheritance. . . . For I was hungry and you gave me something to eat, I was thirsty and you gave me something to drink, I was a stranger and you invited me in, I needed clothes and you clothed me, I was sick and you looked after me, I was in prison and you came to visit me.' Then the righteous will answer him, 'Lord when did we see you hungry and feed you, or thirsty and give you something to drink? When did we see you a stranger and invite you in, or needing clothes and clothe you? When did we see you sick or in prison and go to visit you?' The King will reply, 'Truly I tell you, whatever you did for one of the least of these brothers and sisters of mine, you did for me'" [Matthew 25:34–40 NIV]. To express love to others is to express love to God.

# A Simple Cup of Cheer

*STEVEN L. BROWN*

I carefully parted the curtains and peeked out the window of the warm, dark motel room; I wanted our three young children to sleep just a little longer. White feathers of snow were drifting down to blanket the cars outside as the winter sun began to light the cold, blustery scene.

We had arrived in Carlsbad, New Mexico, the evening before with plans to take the children on a hike into McKittrick Canyon to see the fall foliage. This early snowstorm would cancel our hike, but we could still visit Carlsbad Caverns. A sign on the highway told us the cave was "56 degrees year-round."

My wife and I bundled the kids, all under ten, into their warm coats and blue jeans. All three were giggling about the snow and anticipating the day's adventures. After breakfast, we got them snuggled into the car under a warm blanket. We sang and laughed as we drove through the winter landscape toward the caverns.

The snow blew across the main highway without much accumulation. However, when we turned off the main road, the snow was deeper. A national park service car stood in front of the gate to the seven-mile road into the park. Three rangers were sloshing through the freezing mush. As each of them stopped at the cars ahead of me, I noticed that some of the frustrated travelers seemed to be arguing with them.

When it was our turn, the young man who approached my window was wearing a park service uniform and a standard-issue jacket that looked better suited to the 56 degrees in the caverns than the current 26 degrees outside. Like the other rangers, he was in his early twenties. He looked tired, cold, and more than a little frustrated. I speculated that he was more comfortable with his usual job of answering interesting questions about the park than with today's job of delivering bad news.

"Good morning, sir. I am sorry; the conditions on the winding road into the park are not safe because of the snow. The park service has closed the park at least until tomorrow. You can call the park number for updated information."

"Thanks for telling us. I know it's cold out there. We appreciate your looking out for us."

He looked relieved. "Thank you, sir. You have a nice day."

We turned the car around to head back to the motel. On the way, I noticed a coffee shop.

"How about some hot chocolate?"

"Hooray, Daddy! That sounds great!"

As we walked into the restaurant, the aroma of hot chocolate and coffee embraced us. The tables were crowded with families dressed in winter coats, hats, and scarves. As we sat down, we remembered our motel had a heated indoor pool and decided it would be fun to swim while there was snow on the ground.

I looked back out onto the cold, snowy terrain and realized being together as a family, splashing in a warm indoor pool, would be a lot more pleasant than what those rangers would be up against all day. Then I had an idea.

"Honey, why don't we get those rangers some hot coffee?"

"That's a great idea!"

I ordered three coffees to go and loaded up a cardboard tray with plenty of creamers and sugars. We got back into the car and headed to the entrance of the park. I pulled around the line of cars and stopped near the gate. Coffee in hand, I approached the nearest ranger.

"Hey, you guys look pretty cold out here. We thought you could use some hot coffee."

Obviously taken aback, he stammered, "Well, thank you. Thank you very much."

We watched him through the window of our car as he gave the coffee to his fellow rangers and gestured toward us. Seeing their happy faces was more fun than any hike.

As we drove back to the motel, we talked with the children about how cold those rangers must have been standing outside. We said our gift would give them warmth and encouragement that could last all day, because despite their important jobs, many people did not appreciate the work they did, and even made their jobs more difficult.

Later that day, I thought about the concept of random acts of kindness. Why is it such a rich tradition? Why is it so gratifying when we do it? Why is it so surprising to those it benefits?

If I'm honest, I'll admit that sometimes I have been just as frustrated, and perhaps *almost* as unpleasant, as the travelers who argued with the rangers. We *all* go through life preoccupied with our own plans. We tend to view other people who disrupt us as *adversaries* rather than as those who are simply trying to do their job. No wonder we treat them badly and ignore their feelings.

Why did I take the high road *this* time?

I was in a different mindset that snowy November day. I was focusing on my wife and children. I wanted *them* to have a good time. I was grateful for our time together, even though the weather had already changed our plans once. I was on vacation and didn't have much of an agenda. Perhaps because I was looking outward, I noticed the humanness of those rangers. I empathized with their problems and their suffering. *I saw them as people just like me.*

So many times I see people only in their roles as park ranger, salesclerk, bank teller, or whatever. I forget that they are mothers, daughters, brothers, friends. The lesson I learned that day was that when I interact with people, I need to look beyond their job descriptions and see them as fellow human beings, even friends. I have to realize that they have their own desires, plans, hurts, and stresses. I want to reach out and be an encourager. If I do a better job of loving strangers, they may be more loving to me and to others, and all our lives will be richer for it.

The next evening as we rode home together, we watched the sun set over the melting snow. Reflecting on our weekend, we decided our small gesture of serving coffee to the rangers warmed us as much as it did them.


*"Each one, reach one."*

*"Reach out and touch someone."*

*"Let it begin with me."*

*Over the years, dozens of marketing slogans and even more songs have encouraged us to express kindness, understanding, and even love to others.*

*Our actions don't have to be grand gestures or extraordinary behaviors to make a difference in someone's day. They can be small things, such as a smile, a friendly word, or even a cup of coffee.*

*When we get in the habit and express these light touches of caring, not only do we make the world a better place, but we also make our own lives better. We become more loving people, and fostering such an attitude offers its own wonderful reward.*

## THE 5 LOVE LANGUAGES IN ACTION

Steven and his family were on vacation, but they saw the park rangers as individuals and spoke *words of affirmation*. "Thanks for telling us. I know it's cold out there. We appreciate your looking out for us." Then later they did an *act of service* by purchasing coffee, a *gift*, and driving back and giving it to the park rangers. I'm guessing they were the only ones who gave coffee to the rangers on that day, and one of the few who spoke *words of affirmation*. Most of us have opportunities to express love to people we encounter in the normal flow of life, but often we are so involved in our own agenda that we do not think of loving others.

### LOVE IS A CHOICE

Would you ask God to open your heart to His love and let you be a channel of loving others? Then look for an opportunity to share an affirming word with someone today.

# Drinking Milk with a Spoon

*DORIS E. CLARK*

I've never been to a more beautiful service," my friend Kathy said after the memorial for my husband. "How did you and Duane manage to have such a loving and close family?"

I was hearing this comment over and over. It was true. We were blessed with forty-seven years together, three children in strong marriages, and eight grandchildren. They all produced an extraordinary tribute to a man they dearly loved.

What no one knew was how close our relationship came to ending in shambles one blustery winter evening. That night I realized my love for my husband no longer existed.

*Clink! Clink! Clink!* I looked up from my knitting at the source of the annoying sound. My husband of eleven years sat in front of the TV, drinking his chocolate milk with a *spoon*. I felt a familiar disgust at this habit.

Duane had a practical reason for downing his drink this way. Overweight, he could easily gulp two or three glasses. Using a spoon, he only drank one.

But more than the constant clinking bothered me. Duane was difficult to live with. When not criticizing me, he often sat silent, reluctant to communicate for long periods of time.

He'd changed so much since the Thanksgiving weekend we'd first met. An eighteen-year-old freshman at the University of Portland, I planned to become a teacher and was the least likely of my friends to marry young. At twenty-two, Duane already held a good job and was looking to settle down.

Our chance meeting quickly developed into a romance. School and career no longer mattered. He asked me to marry him on our second date, and I agreed on our third. I quit school, and we married the following April.

The marriage shouldn't have had a chance. We were too young and impetuous.

Our first years together were happy, and three babies promptly joined us. I couldn't remember when things changed, but as I looked at the father of my children that night, the heat from the blazing logs in the fireplace did nothing to warm my cold heart.

Divorce was not an option. No one in either of our families had taken that route. We were both committed to the institution of marriage, even if it had become a prison.

I got up from my chair and walked into the kitchen. *Oh, Lord*—the words silently tore from my heart—*how can I live another fifty years with this man? There must be a way to make our life better.*

Reacting to a sudden urge, I got out paper and pencil, sat down at the kitchen table, and wrote a list of my husband's faults. When finished, I stared for several minutes at the five things written on the sheet. Two of them were truly unattractive traits, one being his constant criticism. I kept trying to add to the list, but couldn't. I felt the deepest disgust at his drinking his chocolate milk with a spoon.

*I don't understand,* I thought. *Why do I feel so hostile over these few things?*

On another sheet of paper I recorded Duane's good qualities. This list was long and included many characteristics that first attracted me to him: a great sense of humor; a strong work ethic that made him a good provider; he put family before anything else; he was a terrific father; and he coached the children in sports. The list went on and on.

*This is a wonderful man,* I thought. *Why do I feel such animosity toward him?*

Comprehension slowly broke through my bewilderment. My focus had been on Duane's few imperfections to the point that I no longer saw any of his positive traits.

Another sheet of paper came out, and one by one I wrote out *my* good qualities. My list of good points was only slightly longer than Duane's list of faults.

Then I tackled my own negative list. I wrote, and wrote, and wrote. And then wrote some more. My pencil traced down the page, revealing many of my flaws. I examined them closely and realized that changes in these areas would make me a better person.

I stared at the four lists before me. After going back and forth from page to page, I could not escape the truth.

*Why does this man stay married to me?* I wondered.

Looking at things in black and white often brings clarity. We both were caught up in a circle of negativity, each reacting to the other. I saw Duane's suggestions as criticism and responded by turning on him. He retaliated in such a way that his suggestions turned to criticisms, which made me even angrier.

I took the list of Duane's faults into the front room and, right in front of him, threw it onto the burning embers in the fireplace. It was a symbolic action. As I watched the paper brown and curl, the last remnants disappearing in ashes and smoke, I put to death all thoughts of the things I'd written on it.

Duane was oblivious to what I was doing. He was still drinking his chocolate milk with a spoon.

Back in the kitchen, I charted a course of action and then began to follow it.

First, I read the list of Duane's good qualities several times and put them in my purse. During the next week, I read them over ten times a day, then once a day the next week. For the next month, I read them once a week. I kept that list for years, finding and rereading it whenever I bought a new purse.

Second, I focused on my own lists. Looking at my good qualities, I realized that I had a foundation on which to build. I went to work changing my behavior on each of the negative traits.

I didn't tell Duane of my eye-opening experience. I think I was afraid that if he saw how justified his criticism was, he might leave me. I also felt that it was more important for him to see actual change in me than to hear words.

Surprisingly, I soon gained new respect for my husband, and my love returned richer than ever. As I changed for the better, Duane treated me with renewed love and respect, and his criticism ceased. I will never understand why, but a week after that night, he stopped drinking his chocolate milk with a spoon!

This happened thirty-six years ago. After that we came to enjoy the deep love that comes when two people grow together for many years.

When I think back to that night so long ago, I know my commitment to marriage gave me the desire to improve my relationship with Duane. But God heard my frustrated cry, gave me the idea to take up paper and pencil, and helped me regain my lost love for my husband.

*The most valuable book ever written, the Bible, tells us, "Fix your thoughts on what is true, and honorable, and right, and pure, and lovely, and admirable. Think about things that are excellent and worthy of praise" (Philippians 4:8).*

*What valuable advice for all of us in all areas of life—but especially in relationships! The old saying "Familiarity breeds contempt" tends to be true. Whenever we live with or spend many hours with someone else, before long we start seeing the faults in that person's life. If we let them, little faults tend to become magnified and may soon be the crack in the mortar of our relationships.*

*As Doris discovered, one way to overcome the contempt of familiarity is to put the faults in perspective—to compare the severity of the negative elements in a loved one's life with the positive attributes that person displays.*

*And then the trick is to close our eyes to irritating factors—consciously ignore, or even burn the list—and focus on the positive.*

*As we consciously look at the good things, before long that's all we see.*

### THE 5 LOVE LANGUAGES IN ACTION

Doris is an illustration of what happens when we follow the advice of Jesus who said, "First take the plank out of your own eye, and then you will see clearly to remove the speck from you brother's eye" [Matthew 7:5 NIV]. When we work on improving our own weaknesses, our changed behavior positively influences our spouse. When we focus on the positive traits of the other person and begin expressing gratitude for these things, we see the power of *words of affirmation*.

### LOVE IS A CHOICE

If there is someone in your life with whom you would like to have a better relationship, would you be willing to follow the example of Doris? First, make a list of their faults and then their positive traits. Then make a list of your own good qualities, followed with a list of your own weaknesses. Then ask God to help you begin to focus on making positive changes in your own life. I predict that your changed behavior will begin to have a positive impact on the other person.

# The Hug I'll Never Forget

REBECCA WILLMAN GERNON

*Y*ou need to spend the night with Daddy, I scolded myself as I drove down the highway. *You always stay with your parents when you go to visit them, not at your sister's house.*

My dad was a silent, impenetrable fortress, hiding behind a stern stare or a curt comment. For most of my thirty-five years I either ignored him or attempted, without success, to have him acknowledge me or my accomplishments.

Neither extreme satisfied me. When I steered clear of him, I avoided face-to-face rejection, but I still longed to have a relationship with him. Often when I engaged him in conversation, his gruff responses hurt my feelings. I felt trapped in a no-win situation.

My relationship with my mother was much different. Even though my parents and I lived 125 miles apart, Mother and I shared our feelings in weekly letters and telephone calls. Mother knew I longed for a better relationship with Daddy but had no suggestions on how to obtain it. Her understanding and hugs helped but did not eliminate my desire to feel close to Daddy.

Throughout this struggle, I harbored a dark secret, one I did not even share with Mother. I was afraid that even though Daddy was older than Mother, she would die first, leaving me to cope with my uncommunicative father. My fear became reality when Mother was diagnosed with bone cancer. The prognosis: three to four years.

While coping with Mother's debilitating disease, I pondered how I would manage staying alone in the house with my father during visits since Mother had been moved to a skilled care facility.

So, on the two-hour drive to visit my mother, I argued with myself: *You need to spend the night with Daddy.*

*Yeah, but I'll be miserable; he won't even say six words to me.*

*A good daughter would visit her father.*

*Maybe so, but he's not a very good father; he rarely speaks to me.*

I thought of the college education Daddy had given my sisters and me, not asking us to contribute a dime.

*Yeah, but Daddy never once asked what I planned to do with my education or what grades I got.*

I had never lacked food or clothing.

*Yeah, but I had to wear hand-me-downs from my older sisters. I never wore the latest styles. Daddy was too frugal to let me dress like other girls.*

I thought of the cost of our family's summer vacations, introducing us to a number of states, parts of Canada, and a wealth of scenery and museums.

*Yeah, but we always stayed in some out-of-the-way place. Not on the beach or in the mountains.*

Every positive thought I had about my father was negated by unhappy memories. While I bemoaned my fate, several Bible verses sprang to mind, among them: "*We love because he first loved us*" (1 John 4:19 NIV), and "*While we were still sinners, Christ died for us*" (Romans 5:8 NIV).

The depth of God's love overwhelmed me. He loved us when we were not worthy of being loved.

Suddenly I thought of a slogan I'd often used when counseling alcoholics: "Fake it 'til you make it."

This clarified what I must do. I would treat my father as if he had been the perfect loving father I had always dreamed of having. No matter what his response, I would let him know I cared for him. I would not wait for his love; I would give mine first.

That night Daddy and I ate the supper he'd prepared. I complimented him on the meal. No response.

After supper I cleaned up the kitchen and then joined him in the living room. We sat across the room from each other reading our sections of the paper in silence. At ten, he announced he was going to bed, leaving me to turn off the lights.

The next morning, I planned to visit Mother at the care facility and then drive home. Daddy walked me outside. Before getting into my car, I put my arms around him. "Bye, Daddy. I love you."

I didn't get any splinters in my body, but hugging him was like grasping a wooden pole; his arms never moved from his sides.

Several weeks later on Father's Day, I had no desire to call my father but told myself, "Act as if you have the best father in the world."

I wished Daddy a happy Father's Day and asked about his garden, a topic that always generated a few comments. He told me about pulling radishes and taking some to Mother at the care center, shooing rabbits away from the sprouting green beans, and preparing to cut asparagus.

"I love you, Daddy," I said at the end of the conversation. Daddy said, "Bye."

Later that week I called Mother. "Your father told me he was happy that you called him on Father's Day," she said.

*Why can't he tell* me *that?* I wondered.

For the next nine months, while Mother's cancer ate away at her bones, I continued my one-sided expression of love to Daddy. In March, I joined him to celebrate our birthdays, which are ten days apart. I looked at his array of birthday cards on the mantel.

"You got a card from Francine?" My older sister had forgotten my birthday. "She didn't remember my birthday at all."

Daddy responded, "What's a card? Nothing but a piece of paper."

"I know, Daddy, but . . ."

"I just said that so you wouldn't feel so bad."

Hearing Daddy explain stunned me. I had always thought Daddy had no feelings since he never expressed any, but under his stony façade he had emotions and was concerned about mine. Now I was the speechless one.

Months later on another visit, I told Daddy, "You know, I really appreciate your paying for my college education. Thank you, Daddy."

He turned away from me. "I never thought I'd live long enough to hear anyone thank me."

All my life I wanted his love and recognition, and now I realized he craved the same thing.

He left the room, and I thought about the number of times he'd done special things for me: buying chocolate-dipped ice cream cones at the Dairy Queen, a special treat that only we shared; giving me a pogo stick one Christmas, a gift I couldn't master so he demonstrated how it worked, which brought laughter to both of us; attending my school plays and concerts; sharing his love of gardening; setting up his telescope to show me the craters on the moon; making a bug cage for me to catch fireflies. How often had I thanked him? Not nearly enough.

Having studied psychology in college, I knew the importance of feeling accepted. How sad that at eighty years old my father—who was a college graduate, a successful chemical engineer, and one of the smartest people I knew—couldn't freely give or receive love.

My plan to treat Daddy as if he was the best father in the world succeeded, despite my selfish motive. Daddy really *was* the best father in the world. He had given me all that he had to give: his love of gardening, an inquisitive mind, and the education and skills to be self-sufficient.

Six months later, Mother died. I continued my weekly telephone calls to Daddy and visited him several times a year for the next four years. Each time I visited, I hugged him goodbye and told him I loved him, and as usual Daddy stood rigid, saying nothing.

The last time I visited him, shortly before he died of a heart attack, when I hugged him his right arm moved from his side and he patted my back. Then he quickly put his arm back at his side. That little pat happened fifteen years ago, but I can still recall the sensation of the best Daddy in the world giving me a hug.

*Human nature often impels us to look at others in our lives and cry, "But you don't care. I can only love you if you love me." Our human nature tends to withhold and wait to give until we're sure we'll get benefits for our emotional time and trouble.*

*But how contrary human nature is to true love! When we long for someone to change, sometimes the best step to take is the first step—acting not on the way things are but on the way we wish a relationship to be. Choosing to have faith in a relationship is always a risk. But more often than not, when we're willing to take the first step, change happens—in us and in those we long to be close to.*

## THE 5 LOVE LANGUAGES IN ACTION

All of us want to feel loved by our parents. The reality is that many children grow up with an empty "love tank." As adults, we experience emotional distance from our parents. Often, we withdraw and simply assume that things will never change. Rebecca demonstrates a better path—choosing not to let our painful emotions control our behavior. We choose to love our emotionally distant parent even when we don't feel loved by them. Rebecca spoke *words of affirmation* (expressing gratitude) and *physical touch* (hugs). My guess is that her own love language is *physical touch*. That's why when her father finally gave her a faint hug she called it: The Hug I'll Never Forget.

## LOVE IS A CHOICE

Do you have a parent or sibling from whom you feel estranged, with whom there is no emotional closeness? Have you "given up" and assumed things will never change? I hope Rebecca's story will encourage you to no longer allow your painful emotions to control your behavior. With the help of God, will you begin to speak some of the love languages to them? Remember, "We love because He first loved us" (1 John 4:19 NIV). The same principle is true in human relationships. Taking the initiative to love someone who does not seem to love you may be the first step in removing the emotional barrier.

# Between Mountain Streams and Ferris Wheels

*SHEILA FARMER*

As the sun rose in the sky, I tried to read but lost my place several times and kept reading the same sentence over and over. Instead of concentrating on the words, my head throbbed with thoughts of *How dare he!*

Just a few steps from the car, my husband stood casting his fishing line toward the lake, perfectly at peace.

A fine mist fell from the sky as birds, ducks, frogs, and crickets sang a marvelous melody, a perfect blending of their "voices." Even the occasional splashing of the fish fit the harmony.

Marvin looked the picture of serenity standing on the edge of the lake, fishing pole extended. While I sulked in the car, he had the audacity to enjoy himself, not noticing how miserable I was.

This was early in our marriage—one that up to this point felt more like a fairy tale and had yet to experience reality. We were at Split Rock in the Pocono Mountains, one of the most stunning and romantic locations I had ever seen.

The setting made me envision every love story I'd ever read, and every romantic movie I'd ever seen came alive, with my husband and me as the main characters. I envisioned us holding hands, taking long walks, cuddling, and just shutting out the world. I wanted to experience the passion and the closeness of a couple so deeply in love they could exchange skin and still not be close enough.

Unfortunately, that was not the same idea my husband had in mind for the trip. On that anniversary, I hadn't yet learned the freedom of individual as well as shared activities.

Through the years, I started to learn about compromise, the mutual give-and-take that makes relationships work. One of the most pertinent lessons came the first time Marvin and I took our kids to Ocean City, Maryland, a renowned beach town.

I loved to get up at daybreak and walk the beach. I reveled in every sound, from the waves crashing to the seagulls squealing. I watched the beach come alive with the rising sun. The dolphins swam in their own little pack as if they were accompanying me on my walk. In the distance, a huge ocean liner inched by on what looked like the edge of the earth.

I wasn't alone in the morning journey; other early birds arrived to begin fishing while young couples cuddled together as the sun climbed.

Later in the day I followed the kids as they raced toward the ocean. I stepped quickly as the hot sand burned my feet.

"Come on, Mom!" the kids yelled as they splashed in the water.

"Is it cold?" I screamed back.

"No, Mom, the water is great. Come on in."

As I stepped into the frigid water, I held my breath. The deeper I went, the more the waves tried to pull me out, the coldness sending shock waves through me. After a few moments of mommy time, I sat on the beach, enjoying the salty air while the sun baked me or my children buried me in the sand.

After a long day of soaking in the sun, we showered, changed, and went to the boardwalk, along with thousands of other vacationers. The warm air blended with the sweet smell of caramel popcorn and cotton candy along the twenty-seven-block stretch. Laughter, talking, and music filled the air. The dark night sky was illuminated with carnival-ride lights. The warm, cozy feeling of walking hand in hand with the love of my life made me want to get even closer to him.

I turned, expecting the same expression of delight on Marvin's face. Instead, I saw that he was frowning, his eyebrows furrowed down under his baseball cap.

"What's wrong?" I asked.

"Nothing," he answered.

The kids were hopping on cloud nine as they enjoyed the best of a child's world: burgers, boardwalk fries, funnel cakes, rides, games, and prizes. Shawn and Shannon made as much noise as they wanted. However, my husband was quietly suffering, all for the sake of compromise and his family's happiness.

I knew Marvin would rather sleep in or fish on his vacation than walk the shoreline before the crack of dawn. I knew he didn't like the heat, so sometimes he didn't join us on the beach. However, I didn't know just how much Marvin really hated the beach in general.

I learned on that trip that he loathed the feeling of sand on his skin. Within ten minutes of even a particle of sand touching his body, he craved a shower. As for the boardwalk, sharing a small space with hundreds of strangers didn't exactly enhance his life either.

He enjoys freshwater fishing for long hours, and I enjoy walking long distances. I could take a little fishing and he could take a little walking, but neither of us could take the less likeable activity for an extended time period. A long walk to him is equivalent to walking to the mailbox, so the twenty-seven blocks of walking shoulder to shoulder with other vacationers must have been to him like a marathon fishing trip would be to me—murder.

I was amazed at this revelation, because although he didn't look comfortable at the beach, he certainly didn't display the misery that I had displayed at the mountains a few years earlier.

Watching Marvin on that trip, I learned that love might mean sacrificing your preferences for the sake of others. Give-and-take is not so bad if both parties contribute.

In the spirit of compromise, I even learned to like a part of Marvin's world that I probably would otherwise never have tried. I get a fishing license each year and enjoy the fishing trips we make to local ponds and lakes. I often watch the hunting and fishing shows on TV with Marvin. I even passed the hunting safety course so I could go hunting with him.

Last season, he took me on a turkey hunt. The first thing I learned was that getting up at three in the morning is hard, even for an early bird like me. But once I had on my camouflage gear and was walking in the woods behind my husband, I found it exciting and relaxing.

We stepped slowly and quietly to a place my husband had scouted earlier, and he managed to locate it even in the dark. As the world around us was rousing, we sat still on two tiny triangular seats in a makeshift tent. My husband grabbed a little wooden box and a stick and scratched several times, paused, and repeated.

The high-pitched sounds pierced my ears and echoed through the woods. Then a faint sound came back. Marvin's back straightened, his lips adjusted, and he made a loud squawk with the turkey caller in his mouth. Silence, then a similar sound returned. Marvin answered the call with the same tone and beat.

The squawk was getting closer with each exchange of communication between Marvin and the turkey. I was on the edge of my seat, holding my breath, and feeling like an unknown language was being spoken.

I looked at my husband, and his eyes shone with the same pleasure that I displayed at the beach. We were in his element, and he enjoyed my company just as I enjoyed his at the beach.

Most people who know me could not believe that I, afraid of spiders, sat in the woods on a hunt. But that is the power of compromise inspired by love: when we give and take, the unbelievable becomes possible and even enjoyable.

*In our idealistic relationship fantasies, we sometimes assume or expect that others have the same goals and enjoyments that we do. How shocking, then, to learn that something that thrills our hearts—like walking on the beach—is torture to the person we care about!*

*When we learn about these differences, we face choices. Some people in a relationship just pursue their own interests, giving each other freedom to go separate ways. Some of this can be good. But on the other hand, it can lead to each person just doing his or her own thing—and that can end up causing problems in a marriage.*

*As Sheila and Marvin found, compromise can make all the difference. At times, they each sacrifice their preferences, to some degree, to please the other. They try to keep abreast of each other's interests and participate enough to understand the joy the other person derives from the activity. The focus is not on doing something they hate, but on giving in a little here and there, being flexible and understanding, and showing a willingness to support the other.*

*Compromise in a relationship is not only a good goal but necessary for the relationship to grow and fully develop.*

## THE 5 LOVE LANGUAGES IN ACTION

All married couples will soon discover that they have different interests. There are symphony lovers and bluegrass devotees. For Sheila and Marvin, one loved the beach and the other fresh water fishing. So, how do we find unity and work together as a team? The key is "compromise." Compromise is not a negative word. Webster's definition of a compromise is "a settlement by consent reached by mutual concession." Thus, compromise is an expression of love. It is essentially an *act of service*. Sheila and Marvin were each serving the other by doing something they did not particularly enjoy, because they each wanted to develop their sense of emotional intimacy.

## LOVE IS A CHOICE

If you are married or have a close friendship, what differences have you discovered? Make a list of these differences and ask yourself, "How have we each made an effort to not let these differences become divisive?" Perhaps your spouse or friend would be willing to do the same, and then have a friendly discussion about the degree of your success. In what areas are you still looking for a loving compromise, and what steps might you take toward greater unity?

# The Little Girl Who Changed My Life

*LAURIE A. PERKINS*

When new neighbors moved in next door, I didn't pay much attention since trees and brush made a barrier between our country properties. But before long I was made very aware of the children . . . one in particular.

My husband and I don't have children, and for years our lives only included the two of us. When I retired early from my job at the public library, I pretty much did what I wanted, when I wanted.

One afternoon as I weeded the kitchen garden, I heard a voice behind me.

"Will you play with me?"

I turned around and saw a cute little girl about four years old. She wore a flowered dress and her feet were bare. Part of her brown hair was pulled away from her face with a rubber band. When she moved, the rest fell around her chipmunk-like cheeks.

"I'm busy."

"I'm Libby."

"I'm Mrs. Perkins."

"Will you play with me?"

"How did you get over here?"

"I came through there."

She pointed at an opening under the trees and around my lilacs that made a perfect path from her front yard to our backyard.

"Does your mother know you're here?"

"She said, 'Go outside and play.' Will you play with me?"

I was annoyed. I had so much to do!

"What do you want to play?"

"House!"

I pulled off my gloves and followed her as she walked under the pine trees that divided our properties. She chattered about where the living room and kitchen would be. She wanted to be the mother, and I was to be her little girl.

"I have to get back to work," I finally told her, pushing my way out from under the tree. I was hot and sweaty, with pine needles in my hair. "I think it's time for you to go home too."

I thought that would be the end of it. I was wrong. That was the beginning of daily unannounced visits at all times.

I was cooking and heard a small fist pounding on the kitchen door. With a deep sigh I turned around.

"What are you doing?"

"Cooking."

"Can I help?"

"No."

"Please. Can I stir something?"

"Why don't you help your mom cook at home?"

"She's working."

"Who's taking care of you?"

"The babysitter."

"Okay." I shook my head in annoyance. "Stir this." I handed her something she couldn't spill.

Each day, if I heard a noise, I would tense . . . listening. Would I be able to continue what I was working on, or would I be interrupted? Each time I went outside to work in the yard or garden, I peeked out the window first to be sure she wasn't around and then hurried into the garden to work, hiding so she wouldn't find me.

When I'd hear her saying, "What are you doing?" my heart would sink, as I knew I'd have to stop what I was doing. Then I'd feel guilty and ask God to forgive my bad attitude. I kept telling myself, "This little girl is more important than my tasks. Why am I so selfish with my time?"

Then one day she discovered I liked telling stories.

"What are you doing?"

"Reading."

"Will you read to me?"

"You wouldn't like my book."

"Will you tell me a story?"

I put down my book.

"What kind of story?"

"A story about me," she hesitated, then added, "and you."

"Once there was a little girl who had a friend. They would travel around the world with their animal companions, Monkey and Eagle."

A little more of my heart opened to her as she listened avidly.

The story of Libby, Mrs. Perkins, and their animal friends was never-ending—with new adventures inside caves, on islands, and near volcanoes all over the world. We'd sit on my swing and I would ask, "Now, where did we leave off?"

She always knew where that was. I especially loved these times together.

When Libby started going to school, her visits moved to afternoons. My husband put a wireless doorbell next to the kitchen door for her to use. One day I showed her how to change the kind of rings it would make. I never knew what to expect, especially since one of the tones was also that of the front door. She and I finally decided that Big Ben's bong would be her own special musical sound.

One afternoon, Libby's sister Katie ran through the trees to see if I'd seen Libby.

"No. Why?"

"She got angry and ran away. Can you help me find her?"

"Is your mom at home?"

"No. I'm supposed to watch Libby and we had a fight."

"Which way did she go?"

Libby had run through several neighbors' backyards in her bare feet. I followed Katie through the yards and we began our search.

"There she is!" Katie pointed to a small figure between two houses.

"Libby!" I yelled. She ran away from us.

I called again and ran after her. When I finally caught up with her, she was crying.

"Libby . . . we were worried about you. Let me take you home."

"I don't want to go home."

"I'm sorry, Libby." Katie caught up with us. She hugged her sister.

I stooped down to face Libby and took her hands. "Libby. The next time you feel like running away . . . run away to my house."

And she did. That was the beginning of years of running away to my house, sometimes in tears. We'd sit in the living room, and she'd tell me what made her angry or sad.

"My friend has a godmother," she told me one day. "Will you be my godmother?"

My heart melted. "Yes, of course."

Neither of us knew what it involved since neither of our families had godparents. But we both knew it was a special promise to each other.

Later, when Big Ben sounded, I was ready to drop what I was doing and see what was in store for that day. Every time we said goodbye we'd hug.

"You're almost as tall as me," I told her.

"I'm only to your shoulder, but I'll be to your chin soon."

It wouldn't be hard for her to accomplish that goal; I'm only five feet tall.

"I'm to your chin!" she exclaimed one day. "I'll be taller than you!"

In time we were looking eye to eye. Before I realized it, she was looking down at me. She'd achieved her goal.

Our times together included visits to our local ice cream store and playing games. Our favorite was the board game Sorry!, which we played at lightning speed.

We celebrated holidays together. Christmas and Easter were our favorites. I made her a big Christmas stocking with her favorite animal on it—a pig. Every year I'd get it out and fill it with her favorite candy. We'd shop for Christmas presents for each other on a Saturday, have lunch, then go home and wrap the gifts. A couple of hours later she would come over and we'd have our own celebration with s'mores, hot chocolate, and a present exchange.

On Easter I would fill an Easter basket and hide it in the living room for her to find. Then we'd take turns hiding the plastic candy-filled eggs.

Each year she became busier with school, friends, and family. Instead of seeing her every day or every afternoon, I might see her once a week or less. We arranged special times together. We drove to a Maine beach where she swam in ice-cold water, loving every minute, while I shivered waiting on the beach. Another time we went to Maine to explore an old fort and ate ice cream sundaes at the Goldenrod in York Beach.

Other special times happened in my home.

"Mrs. Perkins, can we make a meal together and dress up like we're going to a fancy dinner?"

What wonderful ideas she had! We spent the afternoon going over my cookbooks and deciding what to make. On our appointed day, we gathered in my kitchen.

"Here's your apron, Libby." She slipped the navy-blue-and-white-striped apron over her head. I grabbed my red-and-white-striped apron, and we went to work.

"I want to make the dessert," she insisted. I started on the main course.

Libby set out the dishes on my lace tablecloth, put candles at the ends of the table, and arranged black-eyed Susans in a vase.

"It's time to dress," I told her.

"I'll be back in a few minutes," she called as she hurried out the kitchen door. I changed into an ivory lace dress, draped long white beads around my neck, and found my vintage fan. She returned wearing a simple white slip dress and pink necklace.

I fluttered my fan. "Won't you please be seated, my dear?"

She accepted with upturned chin and a twist of her head. "Thank you."

It was one of the most elegant meals I've ever experienced.

Not long after our wonderful meal, Libby came over with another idea. She carried an armload of old clothes, fabric, and a piece of paper with a sketch of a skirt.

"Can you help me make this skirt?" She pointed to the picture. "We can cut up any of these old clothes."

"Did you draw that?"

"Uh-huh. I want one just like my design."

"Without a pattern?" I was being stretched once again.

"Sure!"

Her can-do attitude challenged me. I found some newsprint and we drew her skirt to size on the paper. Soon she was cutting fabric and I was sewing. She went home that day wearing the skirt of her vision.

When Libby went to college, her family moved away. I wouldn't see a barefoot girl come through the trees anymore. Her visits became infrequent. If she was home for vacation and didn't come over, I was disappointed. At times I was tempted to call her and say, "Will you play with me?"

Recently I dashed around the house straightening the clutter and clearing the game table. Pulling out the old Sorry! game box, I gazed at the now-dull yellow cover, smudged from grubby hands, its corners held together with tape. Inside the box, all the game pieces were accounted for. I laid it on the table. Nearly a year had passed since I'd seen her.

I waited with excited expectation. I jumped when the bell rang and ran up the stairs. Flinging open the door, I know I wore a silly smile, but I couldn't help it. I looked at her with so much love. How beautiful she looked in her simple sundress and her long brown hair. She was now a head taller than me.

"Hi, Libby!"

"Hey, Mrs. Perkins!"

We hugged, and I led my twenty-one-year-old goddaughter downstairs for a special time of sharing . . . and a game of Sorry!.

*Sometimes love comes in unexpected packages, at surprising places, and even at inconvenient times. We might be tempted to respond with impatience, frustration, and even rudeness. But those aren't the responses of a caring heart.*

*As Laurie discovered, perhaps one of the keys to finding an enduring affection is to just be willing . . . willing to accept the interruptions and intrusions. As we keep our minds—and hearts—open to relationship possibilities, we might receive gifts and blessings that we never dreamed attainable. Who knows? We might even discover that our lives have been delightfully changed.*

**THE 5 LOVE LANGUAGES IN ACTION**

As you read this story, perhaps you felt some of the strong emotions that I felt. How beautiful to see the results of allowing an interruption to become an opportunity to love a child. Did it require time? Yes, much time, and not just for a day, but for years. However, it wasn't just time, it was *quality time*. Mrs. Perkins gave her undivided attention to Libby over and over again. I'm sure Mrs. Perkins would say it was "time well invested."

I also thought of the thousands of young girls and boys who desperately need a Mrs. or Mr. Perkins in their lives. It is not always the little girl next door. Sometimes it is the girl or boy you meet while working in the children's program at your church or community. Sometimes it is a child in your extended family who has experienced the death or divorce of a parent. Of course, sometimes it is adults who interrupt our lives with a request. Investing in the lives of others is always a good investment.

### LOVE IS A CHOICE

Perhaps you are thinking, "I could do this if I were retired, but my time is needed to meet the needs of my own family." However, if you have children, one of the greatest things you can do for them is to give them a model of serving others. If you are a single adult caught up in meeting your own goals, consider adding the goal of taking opportunities to help others.

Have you had an interruption in the past month that you dismissed because, in your mind, you were "too busy" to help? Will you ask God to help you see interruptions as opportunities to express His love through you?

# Opposites Attract—
# Then What?

*EMILY OSBURNE*

My husband admits that he started doubting our marriage as early as the limo ride from the wedding to the reception. Our driver decided to take the scenic route to the country club and I was furious, worrying about our guests who were waiting to eat.

During what should have been one of the happiest moments of my life, I was on an emotional roller-coaster ride that my new husband was desperately trying to fix. Clay, always calm and levelheaded, encouraged me to relax, but my redheaded temper was uncontrollable at that point.

In fact, Clay and I spent a lot of time during our first year of marriage trying to manipulate each other to act and react in the ways we deemed appropriate. Clay needed me to be more rational, while I wished he were more open-minded and spontaneous. Maybe it's true that opposites attract, but what should they do after they get married?

I am a fiery Irish gal, who was reared by an opinionated mother and an adoring father. Our family gatherings consisted of lively debates. All the grandkids, cousins, and friends filled the house with laughter and loud discussion. Then there was the grand finale of singing around the piano until three in the morning.

On the other hand, Clay's family is much more structured. His parents are polite and courteous, and Clay was taught to be respectful at all times. They are sensible, logical, early-to-bed, early-to-rise, healthy, wealthy, and wise people.

During our courtship, Clay was enamored by my creativity and drive. He was attracted to my positive attitude and appreciated the fact that I always saw the best in him. Conversely, I was impressed with Clay's intelligence and gentle demeanor. He was the kind of person I could trust completely, and I felt a sense of stability when I was with him. It seemed like a match made in heaven.

Those quirky differences that attracted us during our courtship turned into sources of stress during the early days of our marriage. I remember a huge blowup that started over the TV remote. In Clay's family, his dad was the Almighty King of the Remote Control. All the kids and grandkids knew if Granddaddy was watching TV, they were to be well-mannered and watch what he was watching.

In my family, everyone would fight over what to watch and the loudest person usually won. Mom argued in favor of political news, Dad wanted to watch sports, and my brother and I begged to watch sitcoms. On any given night, one family member could win the shouting match for control of the TV.

After being married only two months, I started to notice that Clay controlled the television and I did not think it was fair. So, what did I do? I stated my case for the remote that night. "This is my favorite show, it only comes on once a week, and I haven't seen it since we got married!"

Clay calmly responded that the Braves were playing, and he went back to watching the game. He had no idea of the fury that was about to be unleashed on him at that moment. I have been a part of some very serious shouting matches in my family and had learned from the best. I gave a roaring speech, complete with the heart and passion of a political candidate on the day before an election.

Clay just sat in utter shock, blindsided by my attack. He was not accustomed to this kind of communication. He felt like this kind of emotional outburst was not necessary. I responded to him with a line from *Jerry Maguire*, saying, "You think we're fighting; I think we're finally talking!"

Our patterns of communication were so different that we weren't sure how to move forward in the marriage.

Thankfully, Clay and I had a few important traits in common. We were both extremely determined to enjoy a long, fulfilling marriage, and we were tenacious about pursuing it. We read every marriage book available. We made a decision not to change each other, but instead to seek understanding. It didn't happen overnight, but we started to value each other and appreciate how God made us.

What Carl Gustav Jung said is true: "Everything that irritates us about others can lead us to a better understanding of ourselves."* As Clay and I struggled to identify with each other, we developed a strong sense of ourselves and our strengths.

---

*Carl Jung, *Memories, Dreams, Reflections*, rev. ed., trans. Richard and Clara Winston (New York: Vintage Books, 1989).

We took tests like the Myers-Briggs Personality Type test, Spiritual Gifts test, and Love Languages test in an effort to appreciate our own and each other's strengths. In the process of examining our differences, we discovered more about our personal purpose in life. Surprisingly, we also found a lot of common ground. We both love to teach and have a passion for learning. We are both extroverted and look forward to meeting new people in a variety of settings. We have different spiritual gifts, but we are both enthusiastic about international mission trips and have since traveled together to three countries to build houses and teach English.

I don't think this level of success would have been possible without the help of the many books, CDs, and seminars we incorporated from day one. I can remember sitting in a bookstore with Clay, drinking coffee and skimming through stacks of books on relationships. He would look up from his reading and share a quote from Dr. John Gottman. Then I might find an interesting story in Dr. Phil's book, read it to Clay, and discuss it for a few minutes. It was a cheap way to have a date and learn something in the process!

While reading case studies written by experts, Clay and I were happy to find out that our situation was not uncommon. We are not the first man and woman to come from different family backgrounds. We felt comfortable knowing that we were normal and we could get through this. It would have been a mistake to fumble around in the dark, trying to find all the answers on our own, when they are already out there for the taking.

I am convinced that no matter how different two people are, they can learn to love, appreciate, and communicate with each other on every level if they will take the time to learn about themselves and their partner. The differences between husband and wife certainly set the stage for amusing daytime television drama, but they also provide an opportunity for personal growth and self-awareness.

*Do you have relationship challenges?*

*The wisest man who ever lived before Jesus' time, King Solomon, pointed out that nothing under the sun is truly new (see Ecclesiastes 1:9).*

*And actually, that's true in relationships too.*

*Sometimes when we're embroiled in the problems and emotions of being close to another person, we begin to feel as if we're the only ones who've ever gone through this problem, faced this challenge, or endured this experience.*

*When Emily and Clay began looking outside themselves and checked other resources, they learned that what they were experiencing—the challenges they thought were so unusual—were actually quite common.*

*Checking resources means being willing to be teachable—being willing to admit there might be a better way, and being open to listen to the advice of others, whether through counseling, books, or seminars.*

*When we move outside of our struggles and begin to seek help, we so often find that many people have faced the same issues—and made it through them. And we learn that we can make it too.*

### THE 5 LOVE LANGUAGES IN ACTION

Learning to listen to the views and feelings of the other person is an act of love. Listening with empathy—putting yourself in their shoes and looking at the world through their eyes—leads to understanding. We may still not agree, but we can honestly say: "I can understand where you are coming from." Then you can focus on finding a way to work as a team. You may have heard the old saying: "The key to good relationships is communication, communication, communication." *Listening* is a major part of communication.

### LOVE IS A CHOICE

Do you have a marriage or close friendship in which your differences seem to be pushing you apart? What can you learn from Emily and Clay's story? One way to stimulate growth is to read and discuss a book together. Each of you reads the chapter and then you ask: What can we learn from this chapter? If you are married, I would highly recommend my book *The Marriage You've Always Wanted*. Thousands of couples have found this book to be a roadmap to greater understanding.

# The New Love-Room

*BETTY J. JOHNSON DALRYMPLE*

Friday night! Date night! Movies, eating out, and spending time together.

"Wow, how our Friday nights have changed," I mumbled as I slid a book in the library return slot and walked toward the car.

I opened the door and plopped in the driver's seat, shutting out the cold November wind. I leaned over and kissed my constant companion, my cancer-ridden husband, who had completed another day of chemotherapy. As I turned the ignition key, he said in a low voice, "Honey, I've been thinking. If I don't make it through this, I want you to go on living. Find a nice man and remarry, a nice man like Bob."

"Please don't talk like that," I snapped. "I love you with all my heart, and there will never be anyone else for me."

"You're too young to live the rest of your life—" he started.

"Stop!" I shouted as I gulped back the tears. "I've loved you since high school, and I could never love anyone else. No more talk like this, please?"

I knew why his thoughts had wandered in this scary direction. Several hours earlier, we'd talked with our friends Betty and Bob.

Betty was in the final stages of ovarian cancer, and we all felt the heavy cloud of death hanging over our heads. The dark cloud had hung over Betty's life for three years. And now my husband, Richard, was diagnosed with stage-four colon cancer. Now we, too, lived in the same unwanted place of darkness and despair.

The friendship and love we four shared were like rays of sunshine peeking through the dark clouds of our lives. However, I did not want to discuss any future that did not include the love of my life, my best friend, and my husband of forty-six years.

Two months later, I was forced to face that future. Richard died. It was like most of me had been amputated without anesthesia—except for a broken heart still beating within me and filled with love for the same person.

Desperate for help, I joined a grief support group that included Bob and another woman who had recently lost her spouse. We shared our pain, cried, and walked the path of grief together. After many months, we tiptoed back into the world of intermittent laughter and fun. We three shared a bond, a special friendship, and a comfort that allowed us to step out in new directions.

"I miss my old golfin' buddy," Bob mentioned one day. "Any chance you'd go out and play with me sometime?"

"Okay, let's give it a try," I said.

Bob's compliments and enthusiasm for my game raised my spirits, and we frequently played together.

One night Bob picked me up at the airport when I returned from a trip, and when I opened the car door I found a single yellow rose on the passenger's seat.

"What is this?" I asked.

"Well, I've missed you and wanted to welcome you home," he commented. "Can I buy you dinner?"

*What a caring, kind gentleman,* I thought. Our conversation that night regarding our future pushed me in a new direction. We began spending more time together, getting to know each other as individuals instead of as grieving friends. One evening several months later, Bob rather casually said, "You know I love you."

Startled, I thought, *Love! What does that mean?* Both he and I had often referred to our deceased spouses as the love of our life. I knew beyond a shadow of a doubt that I loved Richard with all of my heart, in my very soul, so what would it mean to say "I love you" to someone else? The "No Vacancy" sign I'd hung on my heart stopped me from responding to Bob. But I asked myself again and again for many days, weeks, and months what it would mean to say "I love you" to someone else.

One time when Bob brought up the subject of love again, I confessed my confusion, and he responded, "At our age, love is different than it was when we were teenagers or in our early twenties."

"It was giggles, excitement, and I-have-to-spend-every-moment-with-you," I said, remembering.

"I believe there is also a mature love for mature people," he continued with a smile. "It doesn't diminish the love we felt for Betty or Richard. I believe it enhances it. It still means I want to spend time with you, and it's saying yes to a future with hope."

I discussed it with a close friend.

"Your heart is big enough for more than one love," she explained. "Think how much you love your children, grandchildren, and friends. It's like God keeps adding on rooms in your heart for new loves."

I could understand and accept that answer. A sense of peace filled my being. And the next time Bob whispered, "I love you," I whispered back, "I love you too."

That was four years ago. Like the yellow rose Bob gave me that memorable evening, our feelings for each other began opening into a lovely bloom. Before we were married, we each honestly expressed our priorities of faith and family.

"It's so good to see you both laughing and happy again," our children unanimously agreed, blessing our relationship.

The foundation of our marriage was a mature love, a comfortable companionship, a trust in each other, a unique bond of shared grief, and a belief that we were doing God's will. We were building a second story onto the rambling ranch house of our previous lives.

Not forgetting our past experiences, we focused on being thankful for good marriages, understanding families, and the wisdom we had learned over the years.

The new love-room in my heart has expanded as we have tried new adventures. Whether it's going on golf trips with friends from my old life or taking a cruise with Bob and Betty's friends, when we extend ourselves for one another, that room in my heart warms.

Recently I was away for a long weekend with some friends, and my eight-year-old granddaughter, Annabelle, told her mother, "Since Nana's gone tonight, I'll bet Mr. Bob sure misses her."

My daughter replied, "You know, Mr. Bob was alone after he lost his wife, just like Nana was alone when she lost your grandfather."

After a few minutes, logical Annabelle asked, "When you lose someone, does everyone try to find someone else who is alone and has lost someone?"

"Well, if it works out to find someone you care about and grow to love, then you're pretty blessed," her mother said.

"I'm glad we found Mr. Bob," Annabelle concluded.

I am too, Annabelle. I am too.

*Since love is one of the most exhilarating experiences a human can have, losing it is one of the most painful experiences. So many times, like Betty, when we've faced the pain of a lost love, we hang out a "No Vacancy" sign—unwilling to allow the risk of another loss in our lives. The numb pain of grief seems somehow safer than the potential hurt we just might experience if we make room in our hearts for someone else.*

*Aren't you glad that our capacity to love isn't limited? What a shame to sit uncomfortably in an emotional one-room shack, when we could enjoy a mansion. As long as we're willing to take a chance, our room for love can grow and grow.*

*Adding rooms to the home in our hearts may cost us at times—we may have to get used to a new way of life, or learn to trust again, or risk losing again. But the result well exceeds the construction expenses.*

**THE 5 LOVE LANGUAGES IN ACTION**

When you have a long-term loving marriage or close relationship, death leaves a hole in your heart, an emptiness that is ever present. It is true that no one can ever replace the one you have lost. The one who spoke your love language is no longer present. However, you still need to feel loved by the significant people in your life. Sharing your love language with extended family and friends will be helpful. A grief support group like GriefShare is available in most communities, and will help you process grief in a healthy manner. Will there eventually be a "new love-room" for everyone? No. That is for you and God to discuss. However, you definitely need friends with whom you can share life.

### LOVE IS A CHOICE

Have you experienced the death of a spouse or close friend? What have you done to process your grief with others? Is there a GriefShare support group in your community? Local pastors or hospital chaplains probably have this information. Have you discussed your grief with extended family and friends? Do they know your love language? Do you know their love language? Married or single, one of our deepest emotional needs is the need to feel loved by those who are close to us.

If you have not experienced the death of a spouse or close friend, are you aware of those who have? How might you help them by letting them share their memories of the past and their present grief? A listening ear is an expression of love.

# Better than Chocolate

*MIDGE DeSART*

How do we measure love? Once upon a time, I measured it by a heart-shaped box of chocolates.

When I was a child, Valentine's Day was one of the most important days of the year. Certain things were a tradition on Valentine's Day. We had a party at school: everyone gave everyone else cards, and we had plenty of cupcakes and candy. And my dad always gave my mom a box of chocolates.

After Mom opened her candy, she let each of us six children have one piece. That was enough for us. What a treat! I looked forward to the day when I, too, would receive chocolates from my husband on Valentine's Day.

The first time my husband, Keith, and I celebrated Valentine's Day after our marriage, he kissed me and left for work as he did every day. But I knew this day would be different. When he came home he would bring that lovely box of chocolates.

To my surprise he arrived home with nothing in his hands. I decided my gift was in the car.

Keith took me to a fast-food place for dinner—still no box of candy. While in the car I peeked in the backseat. Nothing was there.

When we came home Keith didn't mention Valentine's Day. I was annoyed. How could he forget such an important event?

"What's wrong?" he asked, noting my attitude.

"You should know," I responded. Then I gave him the silent treatment.

Of course, I hadn't bought him any chocolates, either. But Dad had always been the one to buy them, not Mom.

Three Valentine's Days later, I still had no chocolates. But by this time, I had a list a mile long of things that would improve our marriage. I hated it when he ate potato chips in bed, and the fact that he knew the make of every car on the road and thought everyone else should know as well. He'd quiz me whenever we were out: "Do you know what kind of car that is?"

I soon knew the difference between Fords and Chevys and what year they were made.

It took me a long time to figure out that Keith was looking for validation. He didn't want me to come up with the correct answer. He wanted me to say, "Wow, that's really good that you know so much about cars."

When he worked on the car, he liked to have me sit and watch. It was his way of saying, "Look at me. I can do something useful and important." I didn't see it at the time because, after all, I was the important one.

When we finally discussed my feelings about Valentine's Day, Keith said, "I don't have to give you candy to prove my love. It doesn't mean anything if a wife has to tell her husband to give her presents."

I thought he was being insensitive. Why couldn't he see things my way? If someone had told me I was the insensitive one, I'm sure I wouldn't have believed it.

This destructive pattern in our life continued until Keith was sent overseas to serve in the war. Our son was born three months before he left. The baby and I moved to an apartment near my parents to await Keith's return.

That year, on a very lonely Valentine's Day, my father brought me a heart-shaped box of chocolates because he assumed Keith did that when he was home. I cried. Dad didn't know it was my first box of Valentine's chocolates since I had married. I never told him. I didn't want him to think Keith neglected me.

Surprisingly, the moment I saw the chocolates I knew I'd been clinging to something that had no substance. The blinders of selfishness disappeared. My ideas of romance and what was proper for a husband to do went out the window. Dad's gift opened my eyes to how shallow my perspective was.

I realized I would rather have my good, stable, loving husband by my side, with or without a box of chocolates. My list suddenly changed. Instead of seeing the bothersome bits in our marriage, I thought only of the good things we had together. I recalled how he showed his love in more ways than I could count. I remembered the first year of our marriage when he nursed me through an illness. He forced me to take medicine when I fought it. He worked every day and nursed me all night. Now that's love. Why didn't I see it at the time?

Keith has been a good provider, a good father, and a spiritual leader in our home. What more could a woman want? What I believed comprised a romantic relationship was a product of my imagination. Love cannot be measured by a box of chocolates.

Now that I'm older and wiser, I know it's important to tell Keith my thoughts and let him think about them. I've learned that he doesn't like people to tell him what to do—he wants to come up with the idea himself.

After I told Keith how my father brightened my Valentine's Day while he was gone, Keith came up with "an idea," and now he brings me a heart-shaped box of chocolates on Valentine's Day.

As I look back on our years of marriage, I realize what a good thing I have. That first year I was no bargain. I couldn't boil water—the pan went dry. One night I cooked something the recipe book called spaghetti omelet. I couldn't eat it, but Keith did, and said, "It tastes good."

Keith is not afraid to change a baby's diaper, do the laundry, or cook the meals. In fact, he likes to cook. I'm the envy of my friends. Their husbands wouldn't think of cooking dinner or doing the dishes.

Now when my husband gives me a box of chocolates on Valentine's Day, I am content to know that the man who gives them to me does so because he loves me—not because he has to.

*How do you measure love? Each of us speaks a different love language. For Midge, chocolates on Valentine's Day indicated that her husband loved her. She expected that gift to reassure her.*

*Her husband, on the other hand, apparently didn't see the importance of giving gifts as a way to say "I love you." Sounds like he showed his adoration for Midge by serving her—taking care of her physical needs and helping around the house.*

*He was saying "I love you" by his everyday actions, but Midge was expecting to hear "I love you" in the form of a gift.*

*How can we learn someone's love language? Sometimes by asking, "What makes you feel really loved?" Another way is to watch a person and see how he or she expresses love to others—and then practice that technique on that person.*

*Love may be a universal language, but sometimes it sounds and looks different to various people.*

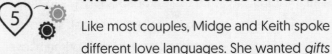

## THE 5 LOVE LANGUAGES IN ACTION

Like most couples, Midge and Keith spoke different love languages. She wanted *gifts* while Keith spoke *acts of service*. It took time before Midge came to recognize that Keith was loving her by all that he did for her. It took Keith a while to recognize how important gifts were to Midge. When we don't feel loved by a spouse or close friend, we should do what Midge did—share with them what makes you feel really loved. However, it should be shared as a request, not a demand. If they don't respond, we are wise to look for other ways they are loving us and give them credit. Then, rather than complaining, we can be thankful. Expressing thanks is far healthier than giving criticisms.

Had Midge and Keith read *The 5 Love Languages: The Secret to Love That Lasts* before they got married, they likely would have discovered each other's love language much sooner.

## LOVE IS A CHOICE

If you are married, can you identify with the disappointment Midge experienced? If so, what makes you disappointed with your spouse? Is it possible that your spouse is expressing love to you, but not in your love language? If you have not read the book *The*

*5 Love Languages* and taken the Love Language Quiz to determine your primary love language, would you be willing to do so? It has helped millions of couples "get on the same page" and speak love in a language that is meaningful. Over twenty million people have read the book, and many of them have said, "That book saved our marriage. Once we discovered each other's primary love language and started speaking it, everything changed."

# Who's Winning the War?

*LAURA L. BRADFORD*

Why do all our conversations have to end in combat?" John growled. "I just asked where you wanted to go for dinner, not which of us rules the roost. Okay, you don't want to go to Andy's Pub because you're afraid I'll keep you out too late. So what's your choice? Should we go to the Dairy Queen, like good little kids?"

My husband stormed out the door for an evening alone at the pub.

*Ouch!* Perhaps I was overbearing, but I figured I had as much right to "rule the roost" as John did. And for all four years of our marriage, I'd regularly reminded him of my "rights." Besides, John didn't realize how terrible it was to roll out of bed for a full day's work after only four hours' sleep. When we went to Andy's, we always stayed until the wee hours of the morning.

Life would have been carefree if it weren't for John. Clearly all men were impossible! I felt women were unquestionably superior human beings.

So why had I married John? I fell deliriously in love with the cutest, funniest guy I'd ever met. John could be the most adorable sweetheart. When we were dating, he impressed me with his strange combination of gentlemanly manners and clownish behavior. He'd run to open doors, then bow deeply like the Shakespearean actor he endeavored to become. He treated me with the respect I felt I deserved.

However, shortly after we married, John began drinking, and the adorable sweetheart turned into a monster. I tried to control him—to stop his drinking in order to avoid his monster side. But his behavior only got worse.

Of course, I was no angel, but I felt my bad behavior was justifiable. After all, I had a monster for a husband! Even though I'd have preferred a stable life with a good man, I'd fallen in love with John. So, I attempted to pummel him into the husband I required.

Our closest friends felt it was just a matter of time before we divorced. However, John and I remained together, even when everyone else seemed to be divorcing. Perhaps it was stubbornness on our part—wishing to prove our friends wrong. But something made us determined to stay married. And something made us fear divorce enough to take a closer look at the dynamics of our relationship. I believe that *something* was true love. When we realized how deeply we loved each other, we began making changes to preserve our marriage.

Lifestyle changes came first. We no longer socialized with friends who were primarily bad influences. Then we quit our high-pressure jobs and moved to a small town.

To my relief, John quit drinking. I also tried to change my behavior, to be more compassionate toward my husband. However, I couldn't seem to get past the idea that our world should revolve around me. Nevertheless, we worked hard to put our quarrelsome past behind us and aim at a "happily ever after." We bought a home and started a family.

Then John experienced health problems. For a short time, his vision blurred. After that his legs became numb and moved awkwardly. His stumbling gait caused me to think he'd returned to drinking, but John claimed innocence.

Just before our son was born, John was diagnosed with multiple sclerosis—an incurable disease of the central nervous system. As we were busy trying to turn our lives around, MS threatened to destroy everything we were working to build.

Thankfully our baby, Danny, came into the world strong and healthy. But John was already limping from the onset of gradual paralysis, a sign he had one of the worst and rarest forms of MS. He soon depended on crutches. My heart ached for him, but I was so selfish, I had little capacity to reach out in love. And I had very little time for my husband, since I was now caring for an infant.

In his despair, John returned to drinking. My lighthearted clown became an angry, bitter jester, wanting nothing to do with a life that had turned so sour. In his misery, John hid behind a bottle, lashing out if I tried to console him. I'd retreat, licking my wounds, conscious of my vast inadequacies.

I felt stuck in an impossible situation—caring for both a baby *and* a depressed husband. I couldn't leave John. I realized Danny needed his father, but I possessed no resources to handle such challenges. How could I possibly deal with all this?

While I was on a frantic search for answers, a sweet neighbor named Mary intervened. She suggested I give God a try.

The thought of depending on a Being I couldn't see was unusual for me. However, I was desperate enough to start reading a Bible Mary slipped into my hands. I'd not been much of a reader, but the book grabbed me and wouldn't let go! It was as if the author knew me and was reading my thoughts. It seemed to be telling my story. It wasn't a pretty tale. However, I was finally receiving a true perspective of my life—a perspective that made me surrender to God.

As I devoured page after page of Mary's Bible, I was convicted of being just as bad a wife to John as he had been a husband. Perhaps worse! Despite intense embarrassment over my errors, something kept me reading that holy Book day and night. It had answers for a heart filled with questions. What have I done wrong? Why do I deserve this? What can I do to help John . . . Danny . . . myself?

Answers would leap off the pages with clarity, even though they weren't necessarily written out word for word. It seemed so crazy. Somehow the solutions were being whispered into my heart.

When I read the line, "Love your enemies, do good to those who hate you" (Luke 6:27 NIV), something told me, "This is your battle plan."

I grimaced at the thought as I studied the bitter expression on the face of "my enemy." As usual, John sat in his chair across the room, drinking, while he glared angrily at a blank wall. Loving him would take far more personal sacrifice than I'd given any-one—ever. Yet as I watched Danny playing quietly at his father's feet, I knew I had to do this. I had to love John despite his anger.

So, I prayed—yes, me, the independent, all-knowing wom-an, *prayed*—for the ability to love my husband.

I started cautiously reaching out to John, self-preservation being my sole motive. Sensing my guarded attitude, John lashed back harder than ever. I realized I mustn't show fear, so

I prayed again. This time I asked for the strength and courage to win back John's heart. I kept approaching him with love and little kindnesses. At first he continued reacting with anger and suspicion, but I kept reaching out.

Then I felt inspired to start complimenting John for his strengths. I determined to praise him at least once every day. Though he outwardly rejected my praise, after a few weeks I saw a crack in his protective shell. And amazingly, as I heard my own words of praise, I began to appreciate John's strong points. He had exceptional intelligence, an exemplary level of responsibility for our family, and a tender care for the weak. Despite his inner rage, John never spoke an angry word to Danny. He was gentle toward our son—ready to listen and to help wherever he could.

However, the limitations brought by John's disease left him frustrated as a father, a husband, and a man. In addition, he carried the scars of deep hurts . . . especially from me.

By then, I'd realized how inexcusably horrible I'd been to John. I couldn't blame him for the problems in our relationship. I'd begun our marriage as a self-absorbed brat. It was shocking to admit that my attitudes about John had actually contributed to his drinking rather than controlling it. The time had come to take my eyes off of me and pour all the love and strength I possessed into healing the damage I'd done. I couldn't do anything to stop the multiple sclerosis, but I could love John despite the disease.

My husband's heart seemed to be crying out for such unconditional love. Though it never came from his lips, his eyes begged the questions: "Do you still love me even though I can't open doors for you? Will you still love me when this disease robs me of all dignity?" I didn't know if I could face what tomorrow would bring, but I kept praying for strength and wisdom.

It wasn't long before I'd surrounded myself with women of faith like Mary—women who knew how to love their husbands and could teach me how to love John. Soon I sensed changes in me. The selfish brat was gone. In spite of myself, God had made me into a woman of patience, faith, and love—a totally new creation. It was *so* satisfying. And by the simple act of loving John, I watched all his best qualities emerge to shine with a brilliance I'd never known.

It took months of consistent kindness and compassion to make progress toward a healthy relationship. Yet as we moved forward, John quit drinking and his anger faded. My silly clown came back.

As the decades passed, our love grew stronger with every challenge. Our battle with multiple sclerosis continued for thirty years. But since I'd learned the meaning of love, I never let go of John's hand. MS gradually took my husband's ability to walk, to sit upright, to use his arms, and to speak clearly. However, as cruel as the disease was, it served as a catalyst to bring out the best in our relationship. It caused me to put my interests on the back burner so I could more fully appreciate the man I married.

Love strengthened John to reach beyond his limitations. He developed into an outstanding husband and father, a passionate mentor to the disabled, and in the end, the most enthusiastic member of our church.

In our thirty-fifth year of marriage, John developed pneumonia. His immune system was devastated, leaving him unable to fight. As life faded from his face, John gazed at me over the top of a large oxygen mask. His eyes beckoned me near. I nuzzled close and planted a kiss on his cheek, then whispered, "I love you, John."

With a weak smile he mouthed the words, "I love you too." Then he was gone.

Multiple sclerosis may have won the battle, but love won the war.

---

*"Love your enemies, do good to those who hate you" (Luke 6:27 NIV), Laura read. How do we show love to someone we're at odds with? The verse tells us implicitly how: "Do good."*

*When a relationship has faced weeks, months, or even years of being battered by the winds of words, negative emotions, and tough circumstances, lip service is not enough. For one person to believe another's attitude has really changed, the motto becomes, "Show me. Prove it."*

*And consistent good deeds give proof of a change of heart. They show evidence of belief, hope, and trust. They reveal that we care enough to put thought into doing little things. They become irresistible heart-candy.*

*Do you have a relationship in which you feel as if you're facing an opponent over dueling swords? Want to instill new hope and life and friendship? Then do good deeds.*

### THE 5 LOVE LANGUAGES IN ACTION

By nature, all of us are self-centered. This often leads to a life of selfishness; seeking our own way. Two selfish people will never create a healthy marriage. Many couples are at war with each other—each blaming the other for their miserable marriage. Change does not come with the passing of time. It comes when one of them has a change of heart. In their marriage, it was Laura who discovered a relationship with God and chose to follow God's way. The Scriptures say, "While we were still sinners, Christ died for us" [Romans 5:8 NIV]. He then challenges us to do the same. Jesus said: "You have heard that it was said, 'Love your neighbor and hate your enemy.' But I tell you, love your enemies" [Matthew 5:43 NIV]. This is not natural. By nature, we love those who love us. However, with God's help, we can love an unlovely spouse.

When we start loving instead of fighting, we begin to touch the heart of the other person. We cannot make our spouse change, but we can influence our spouse toward change. Love expressed in a way that is meaningful to the other person is the most powerful influence in the world. I cannot guarantee that your spouse will put down their guns and begin to reciprocate your love, but I can guarantee that you will never regret your choice to love your enemies.

**LOVE IS A CHOICE**

Are you at war with your spouse or someone else? No one enjoys a lifestyle of fighting. Would you be willing to give love a chance? If so, you can have all the help of God as you become a channel of His love. Would you be willing to follow Laura's example? She found a Christian friend and shared her pain. Then she started reading the Bible and praying for God's help. Then she put her verbal swords down and started expressing love. If you don't already have a Christian friend with whom you can share, I suggest you contact a local church. They can help you find someone who will show you how to walk the road of loving the unlovely. My book *Loving Your Spouse When You Feel Like Walking Away* has helped many individuals discover the power of loving a spouse who is not loving you. You can find it at 5lovelanguages.com.

# The Girl Who Pierced My Heart

*BARBARA L. SCOTT*

The first day I saw her was in late September on registration day at the university where I was on staff. I volunteered to greet new students, but I avoided this strange arrival.

Her head was shaved except for a forgotten lock of long purple hair hanging in her eyes. The bib overalls were at least three sizes too large and looked like they had been favorites for a long time. Scruffy army boots complemented her outfit.

I had never seen so many piercings on one person, and not one of them had an earring. It was as if she were a human pincushion. Around her neck was a dog collar, which matched the chain that hung from the front pocket of her bibs to her hip pocket.

This was a Christian college. *How on earth does this punker think she is going to represent God looking like that?* I wondered.

I remembered my youngest son had worn long hair and shabby jeans in high school. But now he and his wife are missionaries in Thailand.

*I'm sure glad my kids got through that rebellious stage*, I thought, never noticing that pride, along with judgment, now hung around my neck tighter than her dog collar.

During the first quarter of school, I ran into this odd girl everywhere I went on campus. She always ate lunch alone, but I made sure I found other staff members to eat with; after all, she was just a student.

One night my husband and I went out for dinner. An unkempt homeless man was on the sidewalk near the restaurant holding out a cup for contributions. I carefully refused to make eye contact as I walked quickly around him.

Something nagged at me during dinner. Hadn't I read somewhere in the Bible that whatever you did to the least of these you were doing it to *me*? (see Matthew 25:40). I could have afforded to drop a dollar or two in that man's cup. Why didn't I?

Later that night, I still struggled with the issue of loving the unlovable. Whether it was the homeless man or the punk rocker, I seemed to be judging people by their appearances. How was I expected to befriend someone who didn't smell good or didn't dress as I thought they should?

*The outside is a reflection of the inside, isn't it?* I justified. Wouldn't others judge me by the company I kept if I hung around with people like that?

It seemed to me the way people dress often says, "Don't talk to me," "Don't touch me," "Don't look at me."

Or could it mean the opposite?

Either way, I wanted to love as God loves—far beyond appearances into the depth of character. I wanted to see through God's eyes.

"Lord, help me love the unlovable," I prayed as I drifted off to sleep.

"Barb," I heard clearly in the middle of the night.

My husband looked like he was asleep, but maybe he was playing games.

"What, Gary?"

"Huh?" he said sleepily.

*That's strange*, I thought as I drifted back to sleep.

"Barb."

"What, Gary?" I said loudly.

"I didn't call you," Gary answered.

*Hmmm. This sounds like the familiar Bible story of Samuel being called out of his sleep by the Lord. Couldn't be.*

Once again I fell asleep, and sure enough, there was the voice again.

"Barb."

"Okay, Lord, I'll get up."

I trudged to the living room and waited for God to speak, but nothing came. I turned to the one place I knew He always spoke.

My Bible fell open to 1 John 3:17, "If anyone has material possessions and sees his brother or sister in need but has no pity on them, how can the love of God be in that person?" (NIV).

I realized I was being a hypocrite. The unlovable were all around me, but I intentionally ignored them. Everyone has the right to be loved. My love for others needed to be authentic and pure.

The next day the girl in scruffy clothes and purple hair was eating lunch alone as usual.

"May I sit here?" I asked.

"Sure," she responded cheerfully.

"What's your name?"

"Angela."

"I love that name. My husband and I wanted to name our

second child Angela, but he turned out to be a boy." Angela and I both laughed easily.

"My name's Barb. Where are you from?"

"Corvallis, Oregon."

"Oh. We lived in Eugene for many years. Now we live in Seattle, but my mom lived in Corvallis."

It was hard to keep from staring at the safety pins hanging from her ears, and I had never seen a piercing between the eyes. *Wouldn't that hurt?*

Angela was easy to talk to, however, so I began eating lunch with her several days a week and greeting her when we passed on campus. Before long I didn't even notice the piercings, purple bangs, or the oversized overalls.

About a month later I noticed a dramatic change.

"Did someone make you take out your piercings?" I asked.

"No," replied Angela nonchalantly. "I just decided to take them out."

She had a pretty little face now that I could see it.

In November, I went to the big chain bookstore in town to do some Christmas shopping. Angela had a table set up outside, wrapping gifts to earn money for a missions trip. I was shopping for a specific journal for my daughter-in-law in Thailand.

Angela and I were buds now. She knew where everything in the store was, so she helped me with my shopping. We had a good time chatting about school and the holidays. This year was going to be very different for her. It would be her first Christmas away from home. Angela was looking forward to making Christmas special for orphans in a needy country.

A few weeks later, Angela told me she made so much money wrapping gifts that she not only earned enough to pay her way on the mission trip, but she made enough to help a couple of the other students with their much-needed mission trip funds.

By Christmas, Angela had let her hair grow out, cut the long bangs in front, and dyed that portion to match the rest of her natural light brown hair. Shortly before Angela left for her mission trip, I saw her in a skirt! She looked very cute.

I couldn't stand it. I had to say something.

"Angela, you look darling. What made you change so drastically?"

"Well, I figured if I could look weird and you could love me like that, then I knew I could look normal and other people would accept me too."

Angela wasn't the only one who changed. When I asked God to teach me to love the unlovable, I became more compassionate toward the ones I had judged by their appearances.

I saw who Angela was more than what she looked like. I learned to see through God's eyes. It changed my life, as I now see things with a new heart, a heart to see with His eyes and to love all people.

*In her journey of learning to accept Angela, Barbara wondered if the girl was dressing oddly because she wanted to be left alone . . . or because she was desperately trying to get someone's attention.*

*Turns out that Angela's appearance was her cry, "Please, someone love me even if I choose to look different." Those who look like they care least about what others think are often the ones who actually care the most what others think of them.*

*As Barbara learned, we can't be put off by the way a person looks. Looks are no indication of the heart and soul. At most, they might be a way of standing out from the crowd, of saying, "Please notice me. Please befriend me." And sometimes, even, "Please help me."*

*When we learn to love despite the outward appearance, as Barbara learned, we can find a hidden jewel!*

## THE 5 LOVE LANGUAGES IN ACTION

Barbara touched Angela's heart by speaking the love language of *quality time*. It all began with simply having lunch with Angela. But before that could happen, Barbara had to overcome the natural tendency to avoid people who don't look like us. However, sometimes those are the people who most need our love. By continuing to have lunch together, Angela began to feel loved. As humans, one of our deepest emotional needs is to feel loved. When we don't feel loved, we often isolate ourselves, believing that no one could really love us. As Christians, we are God's representatives, demonstrating by our expressions of love that we are truly followers of Christ.

## LOVE IS A CHOICE

Can you think of someone in your circle of life whom you have avoided because they do not look like you? Would you be willing to ask God to give you the courage and wisdom to know how you might express love to them? You may feel that you are too busy to get involved. I can understand that. All of us fill up our lives with activities, but what could be more important than loving others? Jesus challenges us to "love your neighbor as yourself" [Matthew 22:39]. You may be God's agent to enrich the life of someone like Angela, who desperately needs to know that someone cares enough to reach out to them.

# A Wounded Heart Set Free

*AMY CHANAN*

Vile, degrading words echoed throughout my neighborhood. Accusations shot off like fireworks, reverberating down the street for all to hear. Who could say such things to her husband, a man everyone knew to be altruistic and loving?

Unfortunately, *I* could. And I did.

I'm not the type to verbally slaughter someone. I'm typically caring and tender. Well, at least I was until I learned of my first husband's infidelity. The truth of his hidden lifestyle pierced my soul. I grieved with every ounce of my being. But as the weeks turned into months, a new emotion penetrated my heart: anger. I had always supported and encouraged him. I had stayed by his side through the good times and the bad. *And my payback is this?*

The graphic details of his sexual addiction further incensed me. Raw emotions boiled inside as friends and family took his side. *How? Why? This isn't my fault! Why aren't they supporting me?* My indignation kept mounting. I burst in a way that made a volcano look tame. Rage poured out of me.

Nearly a year later, my anger had somehow subsided. Some friends introduced me to A.J., an extremely kind man. We talked casually at a small get-together. A month later, he asked me if I'd go on a date with him.

Fear consumed me despite the good qualities I detected in him. I had once known love, and it had cost me everything. I had nothing left to give, while fearfully protecting the few remaining portions of my spirit that weren't scarred. I tried pushing him away, but he was gently persistent. I finally accepted the date. We began seeing each other regularly, and regardless of my apprehension, I soon found myself falling in love.

A.J. met me at Chuck E. Cheese one night for my daughter's birthday party. After playing games, opening presents, and eating cake, we took Samantha to her dad's house and then drove back to the restaurant to get A.J.'s truck. As we sat in that most unlikely place, our conversation turned to an even more unlikely subject: marriage.

I loved A.J. as fully as my wounded heart allowed, but I knew I couldn't enter a covenant relationship with him until I recovered more from the pain of my first relationship. He graciously agreed to wait as long as I needed. I couldn't offer any timeline; I just rested in the fact that I'd know when it was time.

That day came several months later. Filled with quiet confidence, I looked into the eyes of the one who had so patiently overcome my fear of love and said, "I'm ready."

A.J.'s face shone. As fluffy snowflakes swirled around me and the pine trees faded into the background, I heard a familiar voice ask, "Amy, will you marry me?"

My head stopped spinning as I realized I still hadn't answered and A.J. was about to ask me a third time. "Yes!" I cried out with all of my being.

Four months later, my name changed. I was no longer Amy

Jenkins, but Amy Chanan. I was also no longer the considerate, caring person A.J. had grown to adore. My mind only knew of one way to be a wife. I unwittingly replicated the same poor habits my first husband and I had created. My heart knew that married life did not have to mean constant fighting, but my mouth kept going into autopilot, spewing harmful words at the man I most cherished.

I hated myself for the way I treated A.J. I had a second chance at love and was married to an incredible man, but I knew I would destroy our relationship if I didn't change. I tried with all my might, but voices from the past haunted me. I remembered the numerous times my first husband told me of my anger problem. I pondered my family's words during my angry phase of grief. "Amy, we've never seen this side of you before." "You shouldn't let this upset you so much." "Amy, we're all scared of you." *I guess I really am an angry person,* I finally told myself.

I hated that fact. I taught Bible studies and did community service. I lived a good life, except for my one not-so-secret secret: my temper continued to escalate. I was cordial to strangers, but those closest to me saw a different side, a facet that hurt them and devastated me.

I didn't want to be mad. I simply didn't know what else to do.

During yet another round of anger, I decimated A.J. with demeaning words. I don't even remember why I was upset or what I yelled, but I clearly recall the raw rage and heightened emotion I felt. I was ready for that reckless game of escalation my "ex" and I played for so long. But instead of engaging me, A.J. did the unthinkable.

He gently placed his hands squarely on my shoulders, looked me straight in the eye, and said, "Amy, I know this isn't you.

You've been hurt, and what you're doing is just a reaction to that."

The self-imposed shackles that bound me for so long fell to the floor as tears streamed down my face.

"I'm sorry. I'm so very sorry" was all I could manage to say between sobs. "Please forgive me."

A transformation occurred in me that evening. I won't say I never exploded again or that I suddenly figured out what it meant to love *and* be married. Those came with time. But in that most sacred of moments, A.J. gave me a priceless gift by looking beyond my behavior and into my bleeding heart. He freed me from needing to live out the label I shamefully bore. He repeatedly pointed out my attributes and prevented me from focusing solely on my shortcomings. And he taught me to love others *and* myself.

People ask me how I could possibly love again after everything I went through in my first marriage. My answer is simple: "You'd have to know A.J. He made it easy to love."

*Hurt people hurt other people. The saying is often true. Like a wounded animal, when a person lives in a world of pain, her personality often becomes skewed. She may lash out in anger at those nearest.*

*When we are hurt, it often takes us longer than we expect to recover from the pain and trauma. Sometimes, the least sign of stress or reminder of the painful situation can bring all the emotions rushing back—even though we may not be consciously aware of the connection at that moment. As Amy experienced, we may find ourselves blowing up with anger, fear, or other emotions we experienced in painful situations.*

*So, what do we do when someone we love still has dregs of emotional issues from the past? Perhaps the first thing to do is to remember the pain the person has gone through. That helps us keep from taking angry or harsh words personally. At another time, after the emotion has subsided, we can nonthreateningly ask, "Are you feeling like you're in the same situation you were in before? What can we do about this?"*

*When we truly love, we look at the source of the pain. And though we don't accept abuse, love looks beyond the painful past of the person we love, and into a hopeful future.*

## THE 5 LOVE LANGUAGES IN ACTION

We experience the emotion of anger when someone does us wrong. Anger pushes us to make the person suffer for what they did. If there is no reconciliation, the anger sinks deeply into our heart, and is often expressed toward others. That was what had happened to Amy. It is amazing what A.J.'s *words of affirmation* did when he looked beyond her behavior and saw her pain. "Amy, I know this isn't you. You've been hurt, and what you're doing is just a reaction to that." These affirming words spoke love to her heart. Thus, she responded: "I'm sorry. I'm so very sorry. Please forgive me." She felt deeply understood and regretted her angry behavior.

When we experience angry outbursts from someone who has been deeply hurt by someone else, their harsh words or wrong behavior stimulates emotions of anger in us. If we allow our anger to control our behavior, we will simply be fighting fire with fire. But if we understand the power of words of affirmation, we become a part of the solution rather than a part of the problem.

### LOVE IS A CHOICE

Does A.J.'s understanding words make sense to you? He controlled his own anger and spoke words of love. Do you have someone in your family or circle of friends who has been deeply hurt and is still filled with anger? Could your affirming words be the first step toward their healing? Would you pray that God would give you the ability to speak words of understanding to them? Mismanaged anger has destroyed many relationships. My book *Anger: Taming a Powerful Emotion* has helped many people understand the source of anger and learn how to process anger in a positive manner.

# Just Call Me Babe

*DONNA SMITH*

M y mouth said, "I do." My brain yelled, *What are you do-ing here?*

In a sense, this all seemed so sudden. And wasn't I too old to be getting married? But as I looked into Pete's eyes, I knew that, yes, this was what I wanted—what I wanted with all my heart!

The preacher said, "I now pronounce you . . ."

Before he could finish, Pete grabbed me, planting on me a brand-new-husband's kiss. He turned to his son, the best man, triumphantly raising his fist, a wild smile slashing his cheeks, his blue eyes dancing with tears.

Grasping my hand, he said, "Come on, Babe. Let's eat our cake and get out of here."

*Babe! He called me BABE! No one had ever called me Babe before!*

I watched him, mouth full of wedding cake, pounding backs, shaking hands, looking at his watch, motioning me to *get with it . . . let's go!*

Later in the car, on our way to our wedding night, my mind went in the wrong direction. Widowed two years after having been married to a good man for thirty years, I was now married to that good man's best friend. Pete had lost his wife shortly after my Bill had died, and in comforting each other, we had found our way down the aisle.

Bill had been the perfect father and was a good husband, but was a workaholic, so we had little time for romance. Our "extra" time was spent involved in the children's activities. In all those years, his name for me had been *Mama*.

And why not? I had birthed four babies within five years. After that we seldom had much private time. Ironically, according to Pete, his marriage to Jayne followed the same pattern. So here we were—a forty-nine-year-old mama of four grown children and a sixty-three-year-old daddy of two grown-ups, headed for a night of motel madness.

When we arrived at the motel, Pete unlocked the door, followed me in, slammed the door, locked it, and dropped our suitcases to the floor. He slipped out of his jacket, yanked off his tie with one hand, and unbuttoned his shirt with the other. My mind was a blank. I wanted to go home and hide in a closet. Bill was the only man I'd ever been with, and our intimate times had been few and far between after the children were born—and always under the cover of darkness.

"Okay, Babe," Pete said, his eyes aglow behind his dark-rimmed glasses.

Giggling like a teenager, I pulled my blouse from my skirt and seventeen years of magical marriage began.

Not long after that we were visiting my sister and her husband. I heard Pete call her *Babe*. My heart constricted.

Later in bed, Pete began to snore. I leaned over his shoulder. "Pete," I said. He snored on.

I tried again.

"Rumph . . . mph . . . mmmm . . ."

"Pete, don't you ever call anyone else *Babe*," I said. "That's *my* name."

Mr. Romantic didn't answer, but he'd stopped snoring.

I waited a second and then plopped my head on my pillow, pulled up the covers, and waited for sleep to come.

Over the years, every morning welcomed a dream-come-true day. I found that romance doesn't have to be a dozen roses and dinner by candlelight at a posh restaurant. Romance doesn't have to be expensive. Romance isn't something that takes mountains of effort; it just takes caring and a little creativity—like Wife's Day.

My first Wife's Day came that fall when we went to the Oklahoma State Fair. On the way, Pete said, "Now, we're not going to spend any money. We're just going to look."

At the end of the day, back in the car, headed for home, Pete pitched a sack packed in red tissue paper onto my lap. He grinned like a circus clown, his blue eyes squinched in laughter, his white hair curling above his ears and over the lower edge of his blue denim cap.

"I thought you said we couldn't spend any money."

"*We* didn't. *I* did. It's for Wife's Day. Open it!"

He watched me pull out a brown and red leather billfold and read the little white card, covered with his scribble and tied to the handle of the sack: "Love ya, Babe."

Before I could cry, he said, "That's in case you ever have money to spend, you'll have something to carry it in."

After that, we celebrated Wife's Day so many times and in so many ways: special invitations to supper, shopping trips for clothes I didn't need, craft shows, sightseeing ventures across states, breakfast in bed . . .

I lost count of the times I answered the doorbell to find a lady from the flower shop holding a crystal vase with a long-stemmed red rose, a white card in her hand, biting her lips to keep from laughing. "Is this where Babe lives?" or "Is Babe home?" or "Can you tell me where to find Babe?"

After he retired, Pete would come by the school where I taught and leave notes on my car. Once a student named Sean came into the classroom waving a scrap of paper.

"Hey, y'all!" he yelled. "Look what I found." He turned to me and said, "Mrs. Smith, who's Babe? This says, 'Meet me at Fred's Fish House. Love ya, Babe.'"

The class erupted into laughter.

I reached for the paper. Sean held it over his head. "Why, Mrs. Smith, are *you* Babe?"

After that, he'd yell when leaving the classroom or when he'd see me in the hall, "See ya, Miss Babe."

Another time, Gary needed to borrow a pencil. I told him to get one from my desk drawer.

A moment later I heard him laugh. He held up a pencil for all to see: "Mrs. Smith? Who's Darlin'?"

I grabbed at the pencil, my face burning. Gary held it out of reach. "Hey, listen to what's carved in the pencil: 'Hello, Darlin'.'"

Pete had come to school a few days before and had waited in my room while I attended a brief faculty meeting. While there, he'd spent his time being creative.

After those two incidents, my students looked for more messages left by Mr. Romantic. Though I tried to find them first, many times they beat me to the punch.

We found inscriptions worked in among the notes in my plan book: "Love ya, Babe"; printed in tiny letters on the board under lines of daily assignments: "Hello, Darlin'"; printed on pages of my desk calendar: "Pete loves Donna."

Those mutual searches created camaraderie between my students and me. Still today, when I see a student somewhere in public, I get a wave and a "Hi, Miss Babe!"

Even after all they discovered, though, I didn't tell them of Mr. Romantic's way of expressing love in public, our secret hand squeeze—three for "I love you" and four for "I love you too."

Nor did I tell them that he filled my car with gas so I didn't have to get out in the heat or the cold. Or that he sent me romantic cards for every occasion, even for those he invented: Wife's Day, Lover's Day, Best Mate's Day . . .

The last year of Pete's life, he struggled with lung cancer and congestive heart failure. Because he wanted to be where he could see me every minute, we set up a hospital bed in the living area of our home. No matter what I needed to do or wanted to do for him, his response was "Get on that computer, Babe. Write a story so I can brag that I married an author."

One day as I pecked away, thinking he was asleep, suddenly Pete said, "Hey, Babe, you know what? I have your picture in my heart."

My heart took over my whole body and my throat constricted. I went to his bedside and held him close. I told him I loved him more than anything in the world. I kissed him and told him he was my whole life.

"Love ya, Babe." He patted my cheek, traced his finger along my lips. "Now get back on that computer."

I laughed, went back and sat down, and just as I poised to

peck, I heard a horrible sound. Pete's body was drawn into a twisted shape, his head jerking.

For the next four weeks, I sat with him day and night in a nursing center, under hospice care. Though he never spoke again, once when I held his hand, his fingers pressed mine three times.

Two years after he died, I finally had the courage to open the scrapbook of our wedding pictures. I found a yellow sticky note pressed on the inside cover: "Love ya, Babe."

Pressing that note to my lips, I knew the magical seventeen years of perfect love would be with me forever.

Today, eight years later, Mr. Romantic continues to whisper in my ear: "Hello, Darlin'"; "Love ya, Babe." Yes, I'll always be my sweetheart's *Babe*.

*"How do I love thee? Let me count the ways," Elizabeth Barrett Browning wrote . . . and Pete Smith lived out! Good, steady love is a blessing, a solid core in our lives. But when you top that solid core with romance, well, it's like icing on the cake. Cake can get pretty dry and be pretty basic. But a bit of icing takes it from good to great and enhances the experience.*

*Adding romance to the solid core of your love takes time. It also requires creativity—or a good Google search, so none of us really has the excuse that we're just not creative.*

*Want to enhance your relationship and sweeten your marriage experience? Add a little icing to the cake. Find the fun little ways to say, "I love you, and I like you too!"*

## THE 5 LOVE LANGUAGES IN ACTION

In reading Donna's story, I realized that Pete spoke all five love languages fluently.

- *Words of affirmation*, which still ring in her heart eight years after he died
- *Gifts*, that showed up at her front door on a regular schedule
- *Quality time*, spent on Wife's Day in numerous venues
- *Acts of service*, which included breakfast in bed, and filling her car with gas
- *Physical touch*, in the bedroom and as a way of life

I have no idea what Donna's primary love language is, but obviously she felt deeply loved by Pete. Not all husbands will speak all five love languages. But if they do, they will live with a happy wife. Actually, married life is much easier for husbands who learn their wife's primary love language, speak it regularly, and periodically sprinkle in the other four for extra credit.

## LOVE IS A CHOICE

If you are married, do you know your spouse's primary love language? If your answer is yes, are you speaking it consistently? If so, try asking your spouse this question: On a scale of 0–10, how much love do you feel coming from me? Chances are you will receive a high number. If not, you may ask: What could I do to raise the score? Their answer may reveal a secondary love language that also speaks deeply to them. Add that love language to your repertoire and observe your spouse's response.

If you do not yet know your spouse's primary and secondary love languages, perhaps you could request that they take the free love language quiz at 5lovelanguages.com.

# When Sara Taught Me Freedom

*NANCY PAGE SHEEK*

While I was blessed as a child to have been loved by many, my grandmother Sara loved me differently. Most relationships in my life fit neatly within a set of laws I had either created or accepted—no questions asked. The rules were easy to follow and made perfect sense: If people loved me, I was lovable. If I pleased people, I was happy. If I displeased them, then they were right to be disappointed.

But this was not Sara's love. I knew Sara loved me because she often told me so, because she demonstrated it every time we had fun together, and because when I messed up, she still adored me. With Sara, I was accepted without expectation or exception, so I had no need to please or to perform. I was simply a delight to her, and it felt like freedom. It was easy to love Sara back.

But as I got older, I had a harder time believing all the wonderful things about myself that Sara would say. Maybe I became too busy to spend enough time with Sara, and her voice dimmed in comparison to what others told me. Maybe I was actually more comfortable out in the world because my system was working; I was striving and people were noticing me. Maybe I was ashamed of some of my mistakes. Whatever the reason, when Sara gushed, I deflected her blessings and resisted her praises because I felt they could not be true.

Thankfully, her love eventually proved more powerful than my ability to resist it. Even as her mind wasted away with Alzheimer's disease, Sara's affection would never end, which was very good because I needed it more than ever after my child was born.

When our first child arrived, I named her Sara after her great-grandmother. I had visions of her twirling in monogrammed dresses with bows in her hair. Of course, she would be the first of her peers to talk and walk, and she would delight her preschool teacher because she was so precious and precocious. My daughter Sara would have impeccable manners, grooming, and wardrobe. She would be sweet to younger children yet able to carry on a conversation with any adult in any setting. She would undoubtedly be a straight-A student, president of her class, homecoming queen, winner of the talent show, and a great athlete with a dainty frame. And I would, of course, love every minute of it.

When my daughter Sara turned out to be a child who didn't care what people thought about her, what she looked like, or how she presented herself, I was baffled. For a person who looked just like me, she couldn't have been more different. Actually, when I wasn't exasperated with her, I secretly envied her. I had not experienced the freedom she exhibited since I was a child with my grandmother, yet I fought her freedom with a vengeance. Under the guise of helping Sara be more acceptable to others and appreciated by them, I forced her to comply with my expectations. In reality, I was trying to make her more acceptable and appreciated by *me*.

Whenever I would make her look the part of a perfect daughter, like making her wear pretty dresses and bows, she would balk, and I would shout and shame her. It definitely wasn't the motherhood I had expected, and it left me feeling that I had failed as a parent. Truthfully, what I had failed to do was to love Sara for the person that God had created her to be and not for the person I thought she should be.

"Why can't you just let me be me?" Sara would plead in desperate frustration.

Sometimes I felt like I didn't like her, and it scared me. Somewhere along the way, I had lost sight of the fact that my deepest desires for my daughter had been fulfilled all along: she was healthy and had a sweet spirit that I had wanted for her more than anything when she was an infant. But as she got older, I expected more from her. Now we were both tethered to my weighty expectations, and they were drowning her too. As her parent, I needed to cut us both free.

During these years, my grandmother Sara's mind was deteriorating quickly. I actually thought I was praying in love when I prayed she would die. After all, she had lived a full life with no regrets, and we knew she was going to heaven; surely there was no purpose left for her on this earth, trapped in the Alzheimer's wing of her nursing home.

When I visited Sara, she and I might sit in silence for an eternity, but then she would start talking. Typical of conversations with people who have dementia, Sara and I would talk about the same things over and over. Sara seemed to no longer remember who I was or anything about me, so I wondered if God was really talking to me through her familiar words: "I love you. I'm so proud of you," she would say. "You are so beautiful." "You're doing such a good job." "The good Lord sees you and knows that you are a good mother."

Then the greater miracle happened: I actually began to believe those things about myself again. And that's when I started believing them about my daughter too.

The complete irony of my withholding love from my daughter for not being more like me was that I did not even like myself, especially as a mother. All my life I had loved other people *if* they proved lovable. But Sara lived free from expectations. In fact, both Saras lived free from them, and I could no longer resist either one of them.

For what was perhaps the first time in my life, I would love first and love fiercely, like my grandmother. Coaxing performance from my daughter so I could love her back was not love at all; it was control, and I would have no more of it.

One October morning when Sara was in first grade, I resolved to release her from the chains of expectation I had placed on her. I wanted to consciously set her free to become the person she was created to be. Whatever it took, whatever it looked like, whatever she looked like, I would not fight it anymore.

My track record since that fall morning many years ago has not been perfect, but I can say that since then I have truly loved my daughter. And I like her. She is so lovable and likeable, not because I made her that way but because she was born that way.

Finally, I understood that the familiar words of my grandmother also fit my daughter: "I love you." "I'm so proud of you." "You are so beautiful." "You're doing such a good job." "You will make a great mother someday."

When I started saying these words to my daughter and meant them, they were like a lifeboat for us. I could say I am forever indebted to my grandmother for loving me so faithfully and freely my whole life, in spite of myself, until I believed it. I could say that I owe my daughter for setting me free from the superficial law of reciprocation that I had tried to pass off as love. But according to the love that they taught me, I don't owe them a thing.

*Love is purest when it's unfettered by chains of expectations. The wisest man who ever lived, Jesus, told His followers, "Give as freely as you have received!" (Matthew 10:8).*

*This also applies to our relationships with others. We are each created individually and uniquely. We each have a purpose in the overall scheme of life and eternity. And our personalities—the way we were made—play an intricate part in fulfilling our roles in life. Others who love us accept us and appreciate us—personality quirks and all.*

*As we consider others, we remember that they are created with a purpose. That they are unique. That they are not designed to be our personality twins or our alter egos or other versions of ourselves. Instead, their own form has a function. To love others means to free them from our unreasonable expectations that they should be or think a certain way.*

*Just as we've experienced affection freely given from others, we can free others with our unfettered love.*

### THE 5 LOVE LANGUAGES IN ACTION

"What I had failed to do was to love Sara for the person that God had created her to be and not the person I thought she should be." I think many parents can identify with this tendency. When we do, we tend to speak words that condemn, rather than words that affirm. Nancy's grandmother, Sara, spoke *words of affirmation*, and eventually they reached the heart of Nancy. Nancy's daughter, Sara, was freed from condemning words when Nancy learned to speak words of affirmation as well.

### LOVE IS A CHOICE

If you are a parent, would you be willing to do an assessment of the words you speak to your children? If so, at the end of the day, take time to reflect on the day and write down every word you can remember that you spoke to your child today. How many statements were condemning, and how many were words of affirmation? This does not mean that we cannot correct our children, but even correction can be wrapped in words of affirmation. For example: "Do you know that I love you? I love you so much that when you do wrong, I have to correct you. You are so wonderful and I want others to see how wonderful you are."

All children need words of affirmation. Remember to affirm children for effort and not perfection. If they make a B on their report card, praise them for the B. Next week you may say, "I am so proud of you for making a B. I wonder what you could do to make an A next term? I know you can do it."

# The Good with the Bad

*SHEILA FARMER*

"Tell me something about him that you like."

"I like how he makes me laugh, how good he is with kids, how friendly he is, how kindhearted—"

"Tell me something about her that you like."

"I like that she's loyal . . ."

That's how our marriage counseling session started: my naming a hundred good things about him and his answering with a thing or two about me. Our pastor would ask one of us a question and then ask the same question of the other.

Like so many couples today, our relationship was not the traditional meet, date, fall in love, get married, have kids. Shortly after we started dating, I was with child. With a communication breakdown, we broke up at the beginning of the pregnancy.

Single, alone, and with a baby, my mindset changed to focus on the little life that was now my responsibility. I wanted to have my son baptized—not because I understood the meaning, but because family members insisted it was the right thing to do. I didn't go to church because I never felt comfortable and couldn't relate to the preaching. But then I found a church that was like home and a pastor who preached in a language I understood.

Within months my son's father got back in touch with me and we worked things out.

Before long, baby number two was on the way. By the time our daughter was a year old, we had settled in our relationship, started going to church together, and established a personal relationship with our Lord Jesus. Everything was going great. We had two children, a relationship with God, a church family, and a pastor whom we could relate to on a personal level. That's when Marvin proposed.

I was like a dog wagging his tail when he sees his owner. My eyes saw nothing but sunshine. Heaven visited earth and placed a tall, handsome man in my life, and he was about to become my husband. If being in love blinds a person, getting engaged made me blind, deaf, and—okay, dumb. Not because I was getting married or because of whom I was marrying, but I only saw what I wanted to see: a perfect world of love!

Even with the past problems that had led to our breakup, at that point I only knew we were perfectly in love, with no troubles or faults.

So you can imagine how surprised I was that we had to take a counseling class. After all, we had two children together and were in love. I thought we'd set the date and the rest would be happily ever after.

When my pastor mentioned the marriage counseling, I thought, *Okay, so the pastor will just counsel us—wait, we don't need counseling. We're getting married.*

Then I decided, *No problem—get the marriage counseling out of the way and move forward to the wedding.*

My pastor is a pretty clever guy. I think he was looking to see if the relationship was real. No one would believe it was a real relationship the way I floated into the office.

"Tell me something about him you don't like," the pastor said.

"Umm, let me see, I, uh—uh, well, I can honestly say there is more about him that I like than I don't like."

"Okay, so name something you don't like." My pastor was not about to let me off easy.

I searched my brain for something about my husband-to-be that I didn't like. I thought of making up something just to get out from under the interrogation light. But I came up blank.

"I honestly can't think of anything I don't like about him," I answered with the corners of my lips touching my ears and all my teeth gleaming.

When the pastor asked Marvin the same question, not even a half second passed before he started naming things.

"I don't like the way she _____ or the way she _____ and the way she _____ or the _____."

I could not believe he would say those things to our pastor. I defended all the things he named. Each time I spoke, my voice gained more depth and the corners of my mouth slowly receded from my ears to my chin. Finally, fuming, my arms crossed, my eyebrows crunched together, and my vision returned. He didn't have wings; he wasn't perfect.

"What about your _____ and your _____ and _____," I countered.

I went into the session as a newly engaged woman with the joy of a tail-wagging dog, but turned into a teeth-clenching, mouth-foaming, growling attack dog.

Then my pastor did the oddest thing. He closed his book

and said, "Okay, you have my blessing to get married."

*What?* I thought.

I was annoyed with the entire male race. How could we have his blessing when we were about to reach hurricane-force winds strong enough to blow open his office? And how could the love of my life find so many things wrong with me when I hadn't mentioned one thing about him? And worse, how could he name them in front of the pastor?

I wish I could remember the day when I realized I was the only one in that room with blinders on. I was blind, deaf, and dumb to everything because I was so in love with the idea of marrying the man of my dreams. But the other two people in that counseling session realized that real relationships have real ups and downs. My grandmother would say, "Take the good with the bad."

I think my pastor wanted to make sure we didn't just feel obligated to marry because we had children. I think Marvin, also a clever guy, figured out what the pastor was doing and began answering honestly. It was a wake-up call to bring the dreamy nuptials up front and personal.

Relationships are not the perfect picture I was painting for myself. Matrimony does not mean you get the person of your dreams; buy a house; have kids that excel socially, physically, intellectually; and eventually are financially topped with a happily ever after.

In the past seventeen years I've spent with my husband, I've realized that real, bona fide relationships are successful as two people struggle to overcome their differences for the good of each other.

My grandmother would say, "As surely as you live, you will see trouble some days." When a relationship is built on false pretenses or exaggerated expectations, and trouble arrives, the relationship has no foundation to stand on. Then the troubled relationship becomes like a house built on sand, and when the strong forces come, the house goes down.

Relationships that survive are the sum of love, trust, values, faithfulness, and commitment, but the glue to hold it all together is the ability to quickly forgive each other. In order to forgive, each must be able to admit and accept a wrong. The relationship will flourish when both parties can recognize that they will face hills and valleys before they reach the mountaintop.

As my grandmother would say, "In life, you'll have some good days and some bad days; so you might as well take the good with the bad."

*As long as we live on earth, none of us humans will be perfect. And it doesn't take very long for that reality to become evident in relationships.*

*Sometimes we enjoy our bond with another so much that we only see how great the person is and focus on how much we enjoy that connection. At times it's easy to forget that another person is human. So, when that humanity suddenly rears its head, we can feel surprised and disillusioned and disappointed.*

*That's when we need to remember the wise concept Sheila learned: in relationships, as in life in general, we'll face good times and bad times. Every person has positive traits and negative traits, no matter how seldom we notice the negatives. Love doesn't mean wearing blinders—it means honestly taking the good with the bad.*

## THE 5 LOVE LANGUAGES IN ACTION

The ecstatic emotions of "being in love" and contemplating marriage often blind us to the reality that we are marrying a human, and that no human is perfect. Every couple will have conflicts and will discover things about their spouse that are irritating. That does not mean that we are destined to have a miserable marriage. It does mean that we must learn how to solve conflicts without arguing. Also, some irritations can be resolved if our spouse is willing to make changes. Others must be accepted as part of their humanity. The kind of love that creates healthy marriages is not euphoric emotions, but loving attitudes and behavior. We choose to seek to understand each other's perspective and emotions. Then, we focus on solving our conflicts rather than winning an argument. We don't deny our emotions, but we do not let our emotions dictate our behavior. We solve conflicts and process irritations when we are willing to make changes for the benefit of each other.

## LOVE IS A CHOICE

If you are married, you have likely encountered conflicts and irritations. Have you been successful in listening to each other with a view to solving conflicts? Have you been successful in finding a resolution to the things that irritate you? If not, then it is time to read a book, attend a marriage enrichment event, or see a counselor. Your problems are not unique. There are answers.

Visit 5lovelanguages.com to discover books and events that will be helpful.

If you are single, "in love," and contemplating marriage, don't be blindsided by your heightened emotions. Prepare for the real world: get premarital counseling from a pastor, look for a local church that provides a class for couples who are contemplating getting married, or read a book on preparation for marriage. Many couples have found my book *Things I Wish I'd Known Before We Got Married* to be helpful. In the book I share twelve things I know now that I wish I had known before I got married. The book has helped many couples enter marriage with the tools needed for building a loving, supportive, and caring marriage. You can find it at 5lovelanguages.com.

# Everyday Adventures with Mom

*FAITH WATERS*

Reverend Waters, you've gotta come to the church and get your mom!"

I listened in shock as the woman on the line told me that my mother had gone to the front of the church, grabbed the microphone, and proceeded to curse at everyone.

*My mom?* Surely not! That wasn't like her at all!

When I arrived at the church, she was sitting in the choir room like nothing had happened.

"Why are you here?" she asked me. She had no memory of her actions.

As I led Mom away, I was deeply concerned.

Being the youngest of three children, I have always had a special bond with my mother. She spoiled me because I am her "baby." She has loved me unconditionally.

As a child and teen, I depended on her for everything. But after my father died thirty years ago, she started to grow more dependent on me. My two older sisters got married and moved out of state, but I attended a local college; I did not want to leave my mother all alone.

I loved talking with my mother about so many things, like my latest romantic interest. She often gave me insight that could only come from a wise mother. We went shopping together and spent hours laughing as we tried on big ugly hats and fancy dresses just for fun. We often went to the movies and laughed until we cried. And on our outings, we often ended up at the grocery store, buying vanilla ice cream to share after dinner.

About fifteen years after my father died, I decided to attend seminary in another state. Mom flew to my graduation even though she'd just had knee reconstruction surgery and the doctor had told her to stay home. Her love for me overruled the doctor's orders.

After graduation, I returned home, caring for Mom while she recuperated from the surgery. When she could walk again, I got a full-time ministry position in a town not too far from where Mom lived and moved into my own home.

Over time, Mom started having physical problems. She kept losing her balance and falling. Her equilibrium was awry. The doctors put her on medicine and gave her a cane. Mom did not like being seen with a cane.

"I'm not crippled. I'm fine," she would announce as she grabbed my arm for support.

Then she started to forget things. I would ask about her doctor's appointment, and she would say, "Oh, I forgot all about it."

Now this latest experience was just one more indication that something was wrong. My sisters and I decided to make an appointment for Mom with a neurologist at the earliest possible date, which was two months away.

One morning my oldest sister called me in a panic. Around midnight the night before, her friend had been driving the main highway where Mom lives. He saw my mom walking down the street in her nightgown and slippers. He was afraid to blow the horn because he didn't want to startle her. My sister wanted to know what to do.

I drove over to my mom's house and talked with her. I calmly asked her about going out the night before. She denied it. However, she did admit finding herself on the front porch with her nightgown on and not remembering how she got there.

I recognized that my mother's medical problems were more serious than I first thought. I started spending the night with her to keep her safe. After many tests, the doctors determined that Mom had had a silent stroke, which caused her to have seizures. During the seizures, Mom would lose all inhibitions and have no knowledge of the present.

The doctor put her on medication to control her seizures. Mom did fine when she took the medication. However, she'd often say, "I don't need that stuff. I feel fine."

Then she would have a seizure and end up in the emergency room.

I had to learn to exercise a lot of patience and love with her. I called her every night before I went to bed to remind her to take her medicine. I started going over to the house every other day to check her medicine bottle, and traveled with her to doctor's appointments.

I felt like I was becoming the parent. I was physically and mentally exhausted. Finally, Mom got tired of visiting the emergency room and started regularly taking the medicine.

Just when I thought life was returning to normal, Mom

started complaining about excruciating back pain. The doctors could not diagnose her condition. Some days she felt better than others. One night she called me, complaining about not being able to get off the sofa. I told her to call 9-1-1, but she refused. So I called a neighbor and asked her to check. Her neighbor called the ambulance.

My mother stayed in intensive care for one week. She was put on morphine for the pain. My sisters and I took turns staying at her bedside, making sure she was okay. I often turned toward the window and cried. I had never seen my mother in such poor condition, and having to spoon-feed her broke my heart. Of course, my mom had spoon-fed me when I was a child, but I never imagined I would have to do the same for her.

*But what greater love can a child show a parent than to return the love given to them?* I mused as I learned to take care of Mom's basic needs.

The doctors finally gave us a diagnosis. An infectious disease had invaded her spinal cord system. They started her on a drug regimen through an IV drip. She remained in the hospital for another month.

Because she had to learn to walk again, Mom was sent to a rehab center for two months. I became her coach as she struggled to regain strength in her legs. Every day I marveled as I watched Mom take baby steps and then walk again with a walker. I rejoiced with her just like I'm sure she did when I learned how to walk.

After three months, Mom was excited to come back home. Yet I worried about how she would manage. My fears were soon realized, and it was evident that Mom could not live alone anymore.

I spent four days a week at Mom's house, taking care of her, while working full-time. It became too much. After much prayer and discussion with my sisters, I knew what had to be done. At the age of forty-one, I resigned from my job, sold my possessions, and moved back home. It was hard to leave the life I had built for myself and return home, but I knew this was the right decision.

I immediately had to relearn how to relate to my mother. Our relationship had changed over the years. I had become my own person. You could say I had cut the apron strings.

Mom struggled with the new me but came to embrace my uniqueness. We started to learn to appreciate each other in a new way.

Just as things were starting to normalize, we received shocking news. Mom was suffering from dementia. The signs were there, but I attributed it to old age, figuring I forget things too. She was given medication to help her memory, but the doctor warned us her condition would worsen. It has deteriorated over the last year.

In the midst of dementia and the other physical ailments, I have relearned how to love her. I grieve for the mom she used to be, but I embrace the person she is now. I am privileged to be able to teach, remind, and reveal new truths to her.

Yes, it is tough being her caregiver. She goes into the grocery store with me and wanders away. When I find her, she has purchased five bulk packages of toilet paper, eight boxes of trash bags, ten packs of pudding, and three gallons of milk! I have to lovingly remind her that we do not need those items and return them.

Mom often screams that the television is broken when she has turned it off or cannot remember how to use the remote.

I have to teach her how to use the remote again and again and again.

She answers the phone and tells people I do not live with her. Mom does not remember how to use the microwave, so she tries to turn on the stove to fry a microwave dinner! I have to help her use the microwave every day.

Mom used to teach Bible study at church but cannot remember the lessons anymore. The pastor lets her assist during Bible study and give input.

This is where Mom is at during this part of her life. I can either deny it or readjust accordingly. I have chosen to adjust and learn how to love her in a different way.

The lessons I am learning have forever changed my life. I am no longer self-centered. I have learned how to laugh. I am more patient, compassionate, and forgiving. I rely totally on God for strength. Every day is a new adventure with Mom, and every day is another opportunity to love her.

*People change. Sometimes physical problems change them, as Mrs. Waters's life and personality changed because of dementia. At other times, emotional problems or life challenges make people change. And sometimes people just change because life is fluid.*

*When people change, we might, like Faith, face a decision. Are we going to let go of the relationship? Or, are we going to learn to love the new person who has entered the body with which we are familiar?*

*Learning to love new personalities in familiar skin takes courage. It means not only loving who the person was but also embracing who this person has become. As Faith has found, the process of relearning to love may be harder than we ever dreamed possible. But real love has the courage to continue reaching out through the challenges of life.*

## THE 5 LOVE LANGUAGES IN ACTION

When we were children, our parents (or someone who served as our parents) took care of us. They spoke the love language of *acts of service*. They did for us what we could not do for ourselves. Most of us never anticipated that someday we may be called upon to do the same for our parents. However, the reality is that many older adults will need the help of their adult children if they are to survive. Faith Waters saw the need and chose to honor her mother by expressing her love with acts of service. This always calls for sacrifice. I remember saying to my own mother, "Mom, for eighteen years you took care of my needs. Now it is time for me to take care of your needs." She was concerned that I did not have enough time, or money, but she accepted my love. I provided sitters around the clock for nine years and went to see her regularly. Even in her dementia, she always remembered who I was. When I walked in the door she would say: "My son." One never regrets the time invested in caring for our parents.

## LOVE IS A CHOICE

How old are your parents? What challenges are they facing at this stage of life? How might you best express your love to them? Even if they are not facing challenges that need your help, how might you express your appreciation for all that they have done for you?

For practical ideas on how to minister to a parent who has dementia, see *Keeping Love Alive as Memories Fade*, a book I wrote with Dr. Ed Shaw and Debbie Barr published by Northfield Publishers. For a description of the book, visit 5lovelanguages.com.

# Trials and Errors

*BILLY CUCHENS*

Before I got married, someone told me the first year of marriage would be the hardest. When my wife and I celebrated our first anniversary, I reflected on the year and considered whether or not I agreed. I remembered the first time I saw my wife break down. She couldn't find the cucumber slicer and cried in the bedroom for an hour. "I think you're overreacting. Can't you just use a knife?"

"You don't understand," she said. "I don't want to use a knife. I want to use the slicer. I just want to know where it is. I saw it yesterday."

*All this over cucumbers?* I thought. She was right, I didn't understand.

Several times she called me at work, crying because she'd burned dinner, couldn't find the remote control, or lost her keys. "I have customers lined up to the door. Can I call you on my next break?"

"Don't even bother," she'd snap. Then she'd hang up.

*Great. I get to work for eight hours, then go home and have one of those three-hour talks.*

So at the time, I concluded that the first year of marriage had to be the hardest.

The next year, my wife and I tried to start a family. Becoming a mom was my wife's sole ambition. She knew this from the time she got her first babysitting gig at the age of eleven. She spent her high school years as the neighborhood couples' first-call for their date nights.

In college, she got a bachelor's degree in child development. Armed with a diploma, sensible wits, and a deep love for well-behaved children, she worked successfully as a full-time nanny for several years. Each family that employed her loved her. The kids saw her as a third parent, and their moms and dads trusted her with credit cards. But as she became more a part of each family, she longed all the more for a family of her own.

Considering her skills and passion, it was one of life's cruel little jokes that she couldn't get pregnant. We tried unsuccessfully for a year before we researched doctors.

I remember the conversation we had many times before our first visit to a reproductive endocrinologist. "Other couples are able to get pregnant so easily," she always said. "Why is it so hard for us?"

I finally ran out of responses. At some point I gave up and just said, "I don't know, honey."

The next few months dragged on painfully. Our relationship began to suffer. I spent my entire breaks at work listening to her meltdowns.

"You don't understand what I'm going through," she said. "It's *my* body that's broken, not yours. You don't have to go to the clinic every other day for exams and blood tests and sonograms."

While this was true, it's not like I could do anything about it. I couldn't go through the procedures for her. At times I didn't call during breaks because I didn't want to deal with questions I couldn't answer.

About a year into the treatments, my wife and I went to a marriage retreat where we shared an intensive counseling experience with two other couples. Our first assignment was to each create a life map of our experiences, which we would later discuss.

When my wife's turn came, she shared her story of growing up and how she and I first met and fell in love. When we got to the part about our current relationship, she shared about our struggles with infertility and as usual began sobbing.

The leader asked if I had been there for her in her grief. As I waited for her to proclaim my sensitivity to the group, I heard her say, "No."

"When have I not been there for you?" I asked.

"Lots of times."

"Like when?"

"Do you remember a month ago when I couldn't sleep? I cried for hours, and you just laid there and pretended to sleep. Then when I tried to wake you up so you would talk to me, you snapped, 'This again?' Then you kicked the sheets off the bed and stormed out."

"I did that?" I sat back, stunned.

I tried to remember the incident. If she said it happened, I believed her. I was certainly concerned that I was capable of treating my wife so impatiently. But what concerned me more was that I had absolutely no recollection of this incident.

I wracked my brain, trying to remember when I had been insensitive to her grief. I recalled evenings I had been watching TV or working on the computer when she wandered in and asked, "What'cha doing?"

"Busy."

"Do you want to do something together?"

This question always irked me. It implied I never spent any time with her. Also, it irritated me that I felt trapped by the possible responses. If I said yes, I'd be spending time with her out of pity. I'd be distracted by what I really wanted to be doing. I'd resent her for taking me away from it, and I'd do a terrible job of hiding it.

If I said no, I'd feel selfish for not wanting to spend time with her. One night I got tired of it and said, "You really need to get a hobby."

Now I realized the message I had sent: *Your pain, your misery, and your identity crisis are a nuisance. You need to get over this and move on, for* my *sake, and get a life.*

Was this the husband I had become?

The counselor turned to me and asked, "How do you feel about what your wife said?"

"These last few months have been really hard on us—"

"No, no," he interrupted. "Don't say it to me. Say it to her."

I turned to my wife. "I know these last few months have been really hard for us, and I guess I didn't know how to handle you when you were sad. I felt incompetent because I couldn't fix our problems."

"Why did you have to fix them? Why couldn't you just listen to me?"

"What good does that do?"

"That's how you can make me feel better. You can just be there for me. I don't need you to always fix my problems. Sometimes I do. But other times, I just need you to listen. You have to take the time to hear me out."

"So you want me to just listen to you when you're sad? And that's how I can be there for you?"

"Exactly."

"How do I do that?"

She thought about it for a second. "I don't know. I guess we'll just have to figure it out together."

When we got back from the retreat, our doctor began preparing us for our most expensive and ambitious treatment—an IUI (intrauterine insemination). The procedure's prep included daily injections I had to give my wife in her lower stomach. Also, she had to take multiple medications. She had to go to the clinic every other day for sonograms and blood tests. Her arms began to bruise.

I couldn't get the day off work for the procedure. Later my wife told me how she was lying on the examination table and began to cry. The doctor asked her, "Why are you upset? Most of my patients are really excited about this part."

"It wasn't supposed to happen like this." I guess she didn't know how to tell him that the dream of spending an intimate evening with her spouse and conceiving a child was over.

Two weeks later, our pregnancy test came back negative. We could either perform two more IUIs or move on to IVF (in vitro fertilization).

That night we didn't say much at dinner. It seemed to me that our grief, instead of tearing us apart, had finally united us, and we didn't have anything else to say. Rather than doing anything together, we both just stayed at home.

I couldn't resist the urge to clean. I'd never realized how similar mourning and boredom could be. Doing the dishes and the laundry gave me the control over my life that had otherwise been lost.

I wondered if this was the grief my wife had experienced for the past year. So why was it finally bothering me now? Had I learned from the retreat how to be in the moment with her? Or maybe the treatments hadn't really affected me until now. The doctor gave the IUI a 25 percent success probability. I had let myself think that our year of disappointment would finally change and we would finally get what we had worked so hard for and felt we deserved. Ultimately, I think what I felt that night was my first experience with true grief.

Early the next morning, I woke up and found my wife on the bathroom floor crying. I sat next to her and put my arm on her leg. We didn't say anything for several minutes. We just shared the silence. When she sighed, I sighed. Finally, she whispered, "What are we going to do?"

"We've got to stop the procedures."

"If we stop, then all of our investment in this—the money, the pain, the grief—was a waste. We'll have nothing to show for the past few years."

"I know. But I feel like I'm watching our future slip away. These treatments are like gambling; the more we lose, the more we feel we need to stay with it just to have something to show for it. We've got to stop now before we lose anything else."

We ended our infertility treatments. At the time, I just assumed that the grief and disappointment had finally exhausted us. Years later, my wife told me that she began to heal from the heartbreak when I grieved with her. She told me it wasn't anything complicated—I'd simply made time for her and listened to her and let her vent without correcting her.

I hadn't made a conscious effort to focus on her needs. Rather, I made more of an effort to be involved.

As I look back on my first three years of marriage, I think about the really hard times. I think about the emotional pain and loss of dreams we shared and how these affected me as a husband. But I also see how similar these experiences are to the cucumber slicer and the burnt dinners. In the moment, my wife needs the same thing from me—to listen to her and validate her feelings.

These experiences we've shared have played a significant role in the kind of family I now have. We have grown closer and more intimate than I ever thought I could be with another human. My ability to be involved has strengthened my relationship with my wife . . . and it's helped me be the type of father to my two adopted children that I can be proud of.

*Many of us are created to want to solve problems or "fix" every-thing for those we love. And when we can't, we become frustrated and impatient. Sometimes, if we're honest, we have to admit that if we can't fix the problem, we don't want to be bothered.*

*Love doesn't require that we always have all the answers. Instead, many times love just asks that we listen to the problem, that we try to understand, and that we express our condolences, sympathy, or love.*

*Sometimes love means just being there for the person we care about—trying to feel what that one is experiencing emotionally, listening and learning her perspective until we start to understand and feel compassion. As Billy found, love often means simply "living in the moment" with another person.*

## THE 5 LOVE LANGUAGES IN ACTION

This is the story of a wife who is crying for empathy. She longs for a husband who will try to put himself in her shoes and see the world from her eyes. She wants to feel loved, which for her involves spending *quality time* with her husband. This is hard for a husband who wants to "fix" things. If it can't be fixed, then he would rather not spend time talking about it. Understanding the love language of our spouse, and choosing to speak it, allows us to go beyond our natural responses. Spending quality time requires that we enter into the world of our spouse by listening to their concerns, even when we don't have answers. Empathetic listening speaks deeply to the person whose love language is quality time.

## LOVE IS A CHOICE

What does your spouse complain about? Often, their complaint reveals their love language. We tend to get frustrated when our spouse complains. We often get defensive and respond harshly. Such a response simply pushes our spouse deeper into their despair. How do you typically respond to the complaints of your spouse? Is your response drawing you closer, or driving you further apart? Would you be willing with God's help to change your typical response? If you do not know your spouse's love language, why not suggest that each of you take the free quiz at 5lovelanguages.com?

# It's Not About Me

*CHRISTINE McNAMARA*

I feel like a princess!" I exclaimed to my friend and matron of honor as we discussed my plans for the wedding. At the monthly game night she and her husband hosted a year earlier, I had met Dave. He was a thirty-five-year-old bachelor, and I was a thirty-two-year-old widow with three young children, two still in diapers.

Mutual friends had told me stories of the many women who had tried to win Dave. They also warned that he would never marry a woman with three children. Yet he chose to ask me to marry him! Seven months later, we stood at the altar vowing "Absolutely!" to love and to cherish.

It was especially meaningful that Dave chose to marry me over all those other women, because I had lived with feelings of rejection and inadequacy for a long time. When my first husband died, we had been in the process of repairing a broken marriage after years of hurts.

I had learned a lot in my first marriage and had resolved that if I remarried, everything, including the type of man, would be different. I realized I played a part in the discord we experienced in that marriage, but I believed my husband was mostly to blame.

Dave was definitely different. Unlike my first husband, he had great problem-solving and contingency-planning abilities. I admired and respected those qualities . . . I thought.

After we decided to get married, the plans jelled quickly. We wanted to get married in seven months. I efficiently reserved the church, obtained a choir, and began to gather prices and information about the key components needed for a reasonably inexpensive but nice wedding.

When I felt I had ample information to share with Dave, we sat down to review what I thought were well-developed lists of things I had done. After I proudly presented the information, he responded, "So who has the key to get into the church that morning?"

"Well, I don't know right now, but I'm sure when we get closer to the time we'll know," I replied.

"I think we should know that now so we aren't standing outside the church unable to get in."

"We have months to figure that out. I can't believe you're going to make a big deal about such a minute detail!"

I was frustrated about Dave's focus on something seemingly so unimportant at the time. I was also hurt because of what I thought he was really saying: *You failed at this task.*

Within the first few years of our marriage, we encountered quite a few instances like that in which I walked away feeling inadequate or like a failure.

Once, Dave came into the kitchen while I was cutting a hard-boiled egg and said, "You're cutting it the wrong way."

I asked him what the right way was, and he showed me. I was irritated that he could make something so nebulous a right-or-wrong issue.

Another time I heard the vacuum cleaner and inquired, "Honey, what are you doing?"

"I'm vacuuming our room."

"Why are you vacuuming? Did it look like it needed to be vacuumed?"

"I thought I would help out."

"I do the vacuuming; you don't have to do it for me," I replied, annoyed. I interpreted his saying he would help as "You're not doing your job, so I'm doing it for you." Again, I felt he was saying I was inadequate.

Another example came at the end of a workday, when Dave attentively asked, "So how was your day?"

I shared the frustration I felt with a situation at work. Instead of understanding and listening, he started giving me possible solutions. I thought I was already handling the situation and just needed to vent. I felt he was telling me I was incapable of figuring out a solution on my own.

I knew Dave loved me, but I wasn't feeling loved. Instead, I felt hurt and inadequate. Although Dave was a completely different man from my first husband, I was experiencing similar feelings I'd felt in my first marriage. How could this be?

After repeatedly working through those kinds of situations, I discovered both my marriages had a common factor—*me*.

Through some deep soul-searching, I realized I saw those circumstances as being about me and took whatever Dave said or did too personally.

In working through the hurts from my first marriage and other relationships, I had become accustomed to analyzing how life affected *me*. Blind to the fact that life was not just about me, I was too sensitive to my surroundings, especially to those closest to me. I realized I was an adult, but emotionally my reactions were childish and definitely not beneficial to me, or my marriage.

I was looking for my husband to acknowledge and appreciate those things I did well. Yet Dave admits he does not readily notice or acknowledge things that have already been completed and done well. He is more apt to look for things that need to be finished or fixed. Instead of appreciating Dave's problem-solving abilities, I took his attempts to be helpful as personal offenses.

In each scenario, Dave was only trying to be helpful, not make a judgment on my character or performance. In each, I only needed to hear the information and to decide what to do with it.

Dave's question about the key was a legitimate question. He was merely thinking ahead, not making a statement about my ability to plan. The fact that I hadn't thought of the key at that point certainly did not make me a failure. I could have simply acknowledged the oversight, added the question to my ongoing list, and moved on. Instead, I made it all about me.

Loving my husband includes giving him the freedom to help, give advice, and share his thoughts without interpreting his intentions as personal attacks. Loving him is accepting that his attempts to help are just that—attempts to help. Loving him is taking the focus off me and hearing him with understanding and acceptance. It's letting him know I appreciate his input, and even telling him when his suggestions are useful.

Recently, I showed him a piece I wrote to advertise a program at our church. I wanted his feedback on whether I'd clearly communicated what the program was about. As he read, he began to question the structure of the program.

At one time I would have become defensive, since I had developed the program structure. I would have reminded him to pay attention only to what I'd asked him to focus on. Instead, I listened to his viewpoint and we discussed our thought processes. I walked away from that conversation not completely convinced of his opinion but willing to consider it.

As I thought about it, I realized that he had some good points, and I made changes that incorporated his thoughts. Afterward, I thanked him for his input and I let him know I did implement his suggestions. In this incident, I was able to demonstrate love toward my husband by respectfully listening to and even considering his ideas without making it about me.

Taking the focus off me in these types of situations opens the door for me to more readily accept and overlook Dave's shortcomings—and helps me appreciate and respect him. I am able to love him with a more genuine love.

*The young adults of the 1980s were often referred to as the selfish or "Me" generation. Unfortunately, that segment of the population at that time in history didn't have a corner on the self-focused market.*

*In fact, in homes, schools, companies, and even churches, we're becoming increasingly focused on "making sure my needs are being met." If they aren't, we're outta there—to that elusive person, place, or organization that will be "better" for us. We seek to be served rather than to serve. As a result, we end up always on the go instead of settling down with maturity and letting our roots deepen in our relationships.*

*As Christine learned, "It's not about me." Instead, the best relationships are those in which we decide that everything should revolve around the other person.*

*It's strange, but in life, as the old-timers said, "What goes around comes around." As we become less self-focused and start focusing on others in our relationships, sometimes they start focusing on us. And that's when the roots of love grow down deep, find nourishment, and start to flower.*

## THE 5 LOVE LANGUAGES IN ACTION

We tend to interpret what our spouse says through the lens of our self-perception. Christine lived with a sense of inadequacy. So, in both marriages she heard her husband's words as condemning. She said, "I knew Dave loved me, but I wasn't feeling loved. Instead I felt hurt and inadequate." Her heart cried for *words of affirmation.* "I was looking for my husband to acknowledge and appreciate those things I did well. Dave admits he does not readily notice or acknowledge these things." If Dave had known her love language, perhaps he would have given her more words of affirmation.

Fortunately, Christine came to realize that the advice Dave gave her was not words of condemnation, but simply efforts to help her. The "aha moment" for her was when she realized that "loving my husband includes giving him the freedom to help, give advice, and share his thoughts without interpreting his intentions as personal attacks." He was simply speaking his own love language: *acts of service*.

### ♥ LOVE IS A CHOICE

Do you find yourself interpreting the words and actions of your spouse through the lens of your own self-perception? Could it be that you are misreading their behavior? Would you be willing to replace your glasses with their glasses? That is, to try to look at their words and actions from their perspective? It might be the insight that would turn your marriage around.

# Silver-Boxed Kindness

*PAMELA DOWD*

My husband hadn't been home from work more than fifteen minutes when he said something that poured lighter fuel on my fiery emotions. I don't even remember what he said now. But I *can* recall my response.

Unfortunately for Rodney, I'd been rehearsing a sentence that had roared through my mind like wildfire ever since our unresolved argument about the electric bill that morning.

"I wish I was one of your clients!" I snapped. My palms grew clammy.

I bit my lip. If Rodney could see that the people he worked with got exactly what *I* wanted—a listening ear, a word of encouragement or advice, someone to fight their battles, laugh with, and walk alongside—he'd feel bad about all the ways he ignored my needs.

He rolled his tongue along the inside of his cheek, frowned, and scrutinized me through half-lidded eyes.

"And that means?" I hate it when my attorney husband plays the prosecutor, leading his witness like he's clueless—something you're not supposed to do in a real court *or* the court of marriage.

My hands flew to my hips, and I heard my voice whine, "Then you'd treat me with respect."

"I come home from the war zone to enter another. I can't win." He flipped the air conditioner to chilly as if the heated air between us hadn't already turned frigid.

With lightning-bolt clarity I realized if I really wanted respect, I probably should show some. But I didn't have time to ponder the thought before he irritated me again.

"I'll be at the golf course," he said, and walked out.

Talk about a cycle destined to incinerate the sturdiest of marriages. The more he ignored my needs, the more I complained; and the more he withdrew, the more I punished him. Then he'd complain that I wasn't encouraging enough, and I'd protest some more. Didn't he realize there was no way to encourage a man like him? I sighed. At least our children hadn't been present this time.

I met a friend for lunch the next day. Joy had recently returned home from a missions trip abroad and was eager to catch up. It didn't take long for my marital problems to spill out.

Although perfectly matched to a mellow mate, Joy barely batted an eye as she absorbed my ire. When she prayed for me, I felt distracted. But one thing she said captured my attention: "Let Pam's words to Rodney be like silver boxes of encouragement."

I had no time to ask what she meant by such an odd sentence. I rushed off to carpool. The catchphrase "silver boxes of encouragement" rolled around my brain like a seedling dropped on charred soil; a picture of a different life struggled to sprout.

I decided to find a silver box to fill with supportive words. Although I wasn't sure I'd be able to do it, or find a box, I had to try.

"I want to be more encouraging to Daddy," I told my three daughters when they climbed into the minivan.

They argued that their dad didn't deserve it, justifying my desire to turn back from my impulsive idea. The months of ongoing verbal sparring had gotten to all of us, and I wavered.

Swallowing my pride hurt, but I managed to say, "You don't have to encourage Daddy unless you want to, but be patient with me as I try. This experiment might help us all."

I tried to explain my nebulous plan while I parked in front of a small gift shop. "You want to come in and help me look?" The twins had homework to do, so I plunged inside with my ten-year-old in tow.

"Look, Mamma, there's your box." Lindsay pointed to a lone silver box on a curio table and then dashed to the kids' section.

I found five other silver boxes in the back of the store. I opened each to find a red velvet lining. I frowned. Something about the color red reminded me of what I'd be giving up by changing—the *power* to harp and complain, the *right* to take his bait and react with vengeance, the *entitlement* that shouted I didn't deserve to be treated this way.

I shook my head. I was as filled with ugly thinking as my husband was with unbridled anger.

I returned to examine the box my daughter had picked out. This little treasure box had white velvet lining that reminded me of what I wanted my words to represent: sincere kindness.

When we got home, I placed the box on my bathroom counter beneath the mirror. That might sound silly, but I figured I'd have to practice saying anything I came up with. The situation was that bad between us. The task of encouraging a man who'd made my life miserable took on the proportions of a miracle. I tapped my pencil, pondering what to say. What sincere compliment could I offer?

I finally wrote on a strip of paper: "I appreciate it when you fill up the gas tank."

I slipped the sentence into the box and decided to tell Rodney when we were all alone. I didn't want to see the girls rolling their eyes.

I spoke the simple words with a pounding heart. He said, "Thank you for noticing."

Wow. My skin tingled.

As I slid beneath the comforter to read a verse or two from the Bible before bed, I found Ephesians 4:29: "Let everything you say be good and helpful, so that your words will be an encouragement to those who hear them." I smiled as I drifted off to sleep with a *thank-you* winging heavenward.

Throughout the next year, I filled the silver box with many encouraging words. Rodney had no idea what I was doing, but his attitude changed, and he seemed to gain more confidence. The girls noticed too. Peace had entered our home.

I spoke and wrote until the sentences popped out of the box like springy jack-in-the-box papers. It was heartening to watch my experiment grow.

When I got discouraged, I would reread my positive comments to bolster my resolve. As I practiced dispensing encouragement, it became more ingrained.

On New Year's Day, I presented the silver box to Rodney. He painstakingly opened each narrow strip of paper—at least two hundred. He read them aloud, stunned. He hadn't realized I'd been filling a box, but he had noticed *I'd* changed!

*Words are powerful and compliments are strong. The Bible even talks about words well spoken being like "golden apples in a silver basket" (Proverbs 25:11). Gold and silver are not only precious metals but also valuable.*

*Likewise, complimentary words are not only precious but valuable. One sweet comment may not make a lot of difference, but add up enough of them—at least one a day—and they can stem the negative tide in a relationship and even change the direction.*

*The key, as Pamela pointed out, is sincerity. When we're just flattering someone, they usually see through it or mistrust the lack of honesty they sense. But when we're vulnerable, specific, and truthful, our words are appreciated.*

*Don't know where to start in bringing compliments into a relationship? Well, something as basic as "I appreciate it when you fill up the gas tank," as Pamela found, works just fine.*

### THE 5 LOVE LANGUAGES IN ACTION

Pamela traded in verbal bombs for verbal balms. Critical words always push our spouse further away. Rodney chose to be on the golf course rather than in the house with a critical wife. The Scriptures say: "The tongue has the power of life and death" [Proverbs 18:21 NIV]. When Pamela learned the positive results of speaking *words of affirmation* to her husband, she was giving life to her marriage. My guess is that she was speaking his love language. Critical words are painful to anyone, but to someone whose love language is *words of affirmation*, they are like a dagger to the heart. We don't choose our emotions, but we do choose our words.

### LOVE IS A CHOICE

Would you be willing to keep a record of the words you say to your spouse tomorrow? Write them under two columns: Positive and Negative or Affirming and Critical. You might be surprised at what you discover. If you lean toward the critical side, you might want to set a goal of speaking at least one affirming word each day. You may want to get your own silver box and fill it with words that give life.

# A Spring Tulip in Frozen Ground

*GENA BRADFORD*

When I was twenty-one, I married my best friend, Jack. We met at college. I loved him for his good sense of humor, his wit, and his easygoing personality. He was voted class clown, and daily he made me laugh out loud. It was his trademark. He also seemed stable and faithful, two qualities I counted most valuable since I grew up in a broken home. I thought my love for him would last forever, but we were young and our love was built on the unrealistic expectations we had for each other.

At the seven-year mark of our marriage, I watched my husband's personality change from a self-confident man of great charm to an unhappy man, a difficult-to-live-with stranger. And as he changed, I found myself losing my love for him.

We had just moved from California back to our college town of Spokane, Washington, planning to raise our young family there. Although Jack didn't have a job, we had saved enough money for several weeks' living expenses and felt confident that he would find a job soon.

We were wrong.

"You're overeducated," employer after employer told him, looking at his two degrees in psychology and theology. There were no openings where he could utilize his academic training. Employers in blue-collar jobs were reluctant to hire him, afraid he'd leave when something better opened up.

As employment doors continued to close, Jack withdrew deeper into himself. He'd roam restlessly around the house brooding, not talking to any of us.

When our three-year-old daughter would ask, "Daddy, please play with me," he'd snap at her, "Don't bother me, I'm thinking." Her daddy's behavior confused her. Normally he loved to romp and play with her.

When I'd ask, "Do you want to talk about what's bothering you?" I'd get a curt brush-off: "Nothing's bothering me" or "I don't want to talk."

When I suggested something the family could do together, like a picnic in the park, he'd respond, "I'd rather not . . . go by yourselves." Always a whistler, he even stopped that. He just brooded in introspective silence.

I began to respond to Jack's bad moods. They made me angry. I started giving him all kinds of advice about how he could find work.

"Honey," I said to him one day, "why don't you sell vacuum cleaners? They're always looking for sales representatives."

Yet as I said it, I knew full well he had a phobia about that kind of door-to-door selling.

I gave him all kinds of spiritual advice too. "You're trying to carry this all by yourself," I'd say, expecting him to "rest in the Lord," and to enjoy each day with the family.

As weeks dragged into months, I became disgusted with his behavior. Jack was no longer the joyful, loving man I had married. An icy distance grew wider and wider between us, and to make matters worse, we fell two months behind in the rent. Our savings were all gone.

Now I felt helplessly trapped. I kept trying to blot out the ugly thought of divorce. I didn't want to leave Jack, but I also didn't want to stay with him. The very idea of divorce saddened me. My mother had been married three times, and I lived with the memory of a premarital counselor warning me that statistically I, too, was a divorce risk. "It's almost inevitable for you," he had said.

To me, divorce seemed like a kind of death, a black empty room with no light or life. I'd experienced its pain too much with my own parents, and yet I couldn't imagine living for a lifetime with someone I didn't love.

One afternoon when I felt at my lowest ebb, my next-door neighbor dropped in. I'd enjoyed wonderful over-the-fence conversations with Peg. She'd been married many years, and we often shared our thoughts on family and faith. She had become a motherly presence for me.

We sat at the kitchen table. I poured cups of tea. There was a silence. Then Peg spoke: "How are you doing, Gena? How are you really doing?"

Something in her gentle tone triggered my pent-up feelings. I blurted out, "I don't know what I'm going to do, Peg. I don't love Jack anymore!"

"Oh, that," she replied calmly. I felt hurt at the matter-of-fact way she took my startling confession.

Peg put her hand on mine. "Gena, I've been watching you two young people. What you are feeling about Jack is nothing unexpected, or new. It's happened to me and many other women as well."

"But this is different," I protested.

"No, my dear, I'm afraid it's not." And then Peg began to give me the wisest lesson in loving that I'd ever heard. "Human love is a living thing, always changing," she began. "It changes as we change, and sometimes we shape it ourselves. We put conditions on it, such as 'I'll love you if you meet my expectations.'"

As she talked I began to wonder, had I lost my love for Jack because he was no longer the cheerful man I'd married?

"But there's one love that doesn't change," Peg added. "And that's the one you have to bring into your marriage now."

"What love is that?" I asked, a little bewildered.

"It's God's resurrection love. When our human love dies, He can replace it with divine love."

Before Peg went home that day, she urged me to pray and ask God for His love for Jack, but first I must be willing to trust Him, to wait to see what He could do. She encouraged me to see Jack as God sees him, with understanding, tenderness, forbearance, and forgiveness.

As soon as Peg left for home, I spoke out loud the simplest prayer, "God, I ask You to give me Your love for Jack."

A few hours later, Jack came home, his face revealing the discouragement of his day. *Who has turned him down this time?* I wondered. *What kind of painful rejection is he feeling now?*

For the first time in weeks I looked at him without trying to avoid his eyes, and as I did, I felt a little surge of warmth, like a blade of a green spring tulip forcing its way from the frozen ground of winter.

From that day on, it seemed to me that Jack began to change.

What I didn't grasp then, however, was that *I* was the one who was changing. I stopped trying to exert my will on him, stopped trying to make him meet my expectations. I left him to find his own way while I stopped the nagging. I concentrated on taking good care of the children and doing my best to say and think only genuinely supportive things. And I prayed often to God that He would watch over my husband.

About a week later, when we were down to our very last five dollars, Jack unexpectedly called the children and me into the living room. We gathered around the fireplace.

"I want to read something to you," he explained, "and tell you what I've done." As I sat with our one-year-old squirming on my lap, he read to us the passage in Matthew 6:25–26 that says, "Do not worry about your life, what you will eat . . ." (NIV), and continues with the assurance that if God cares for the birds of the air, surely He will care for us.

"I told God," Jack said, "that since this is His promise to us, I must believe He will take care of me and my family. I've tried with my own strength to find a job using every avenue I know. I've found nothing and have no prospects."

"Well, God," Jack continued, "I trust You now to do what's best for all of us. Until You do, I'm going to pretend that I'm on vacation and enjoy the time with my family."

And with that announcement he looked around at us and smiled, really smiled, for the first time in months!

The next morning, buoyant with his conviction of God's loving care, Jack decided to look once more for work. He told us later that as he drove toward town, he prayed again, "God, please guide me. I don't know where else to go." At that very moment, his eyes were drawn to a sign advertising the one employment agency he hadn't visited. He entered the office and behind the main desk found a college friend he hadn't seen for years.

After he poured out the story of his frustrating search for work, his friend told him about an entry-level job with the state of Washington. Jack was hired. It was a low-paying job, but it was a job, and Jack gave all his energy to it. Within three years, his responsibilities and salary had tripled.

Jack stayed with state work for thirty-six years, supporting his growing family of four children through college and into careers of their own. He was promoted to a job within the state that used his degrees earned in college. To this day, he counsels men in recovery.

We are now grandparents! We are also enjoying a relationship with each other far better than ever. The love and joy, the humor and faithfulness, have come from the knowledge of God's unconditional love for both of us and from the lessons we've learned about showing grace to each other, forgiving one another because we are forgiven by God. All we needed to do was ask the Father of life to take a dead relationship and make something brand-new.

Together we have experienced the supernatural power of God's resurrection love, a love that has grown through all the years of our marriage. Each trial became an opportunity to learn to love God's way.

Just when you think love is at an end, that's the time to really start loving. As Peg would say, that's the time to tap into the love that is always there and never changes—God's love.

*Relationships, like life in general, go through seasons. Sometimes we're in arid summer seasons, when our relationships seem dry and in need of some nurturing rain. Sometimes we go through harvest times of plenty, when feasting and thankfulness are in order. At other times, our relationships are cold, and it's hard to keep the flames fanned. Sometimes we even think our friendships or relationships are facing a wintry death.*

*But like a plant that bursts from the cold ground grows and blooms every spring, if we have planted love, we can be sure our relationships will eventually find new life. Sometimes it just means hanging in there during the cold, dark days when we forget what the warmth of life is like.*

*If you're feeling the icy winds, hang on with love . . . soon the season will change.*

### THE 5 LOVE LANGUAGES IN ACTION

Sometimes in our discouragement, we isolate ourselves from family who may be trying to help us. We may also question why God is allowing the things that have come our way. When a spouse feels rejected, emotions of love evaporate. Neither of us feel supported by the other, and we sometimes come to resent each other. In these dark valleys of the soul, we sometimes feel like giving up.

It is in these seasons we need to hear and receive the love of God. When Gena turned her heart toward God and asked Him to let her express His love for Jack, things began to change. She said, "I stopped trying to exert my will on him, stopped trying to make him meet my expectations. I stopped the nagging, and did my best to say and think only genuinely supportive things. I prayed often to God that He would watch over my husband." When Jack turned to God's Word, he heard the promise of God to take care of him and his family. He put his trust in God, and his attitude, emotions, and behavior began to change. Receiving God's love and putting our trust in Him rather than self-effort is the road to reconciliation.

### LOVE IS A CHOICE

God wants to pour His love into our hearts. When we open our hearts to receive His love, all of life looks different. We then become channels of expressing His love to others. Nothing is more satisfying than letting God use us to enrich the lives of others. If you have never read my book *God Speaks Your Love Language*, I think you will find it helpful.

# All She Needed Was Time

*KATHERINE J. CRAWFORD*

On our twenty-fifth wedding anniversary, my husband left me alone to care for his ninety-three-year-old mother. She had lived in our home for two years, and some days were easier than others. When I delivered her breakfast to her room, I checked her bedding and snagged her dirty pants from the chair before she could put them on again.

"Grandma, it's just an hour until the visiting nurse comes. She'll help you bathe."

"I don't need anyone to help me," she snarled at me. "If you hadn't tricked my son into marrying you, I wouldn't be here."

Tears filled my eyes. I turned my back on the angry, white-haired woman and opened her closet. "I washed your lavender dress yesterday. Do you want to wear it or the pink one?"

"I told everyone if you were good to me, I'd give you my tablecloth. Well, no daughter-in-law is ever going to treat me this way. You can't make me have a bath."

I didn't stay to listen to the rest of her tirade. I scooted into the bathroom before tears of self-pity rained down my face.

"Lord, I've done everything to make that woman like me. What do I do now?"

Before long, I'd mopped my face, retouched my makeup, and met the nurse at the back door. I used her visit as an opportunity to run an errand and tried to leave the cloud of depression behind.

At the store, my friend Tammy's cheerfulness brought a fresh bucket of tears.

"Good morning, Kathy. How are things with Grandma?" She handed me a tissue and said, "That bad?"

"Married twenty-five years today, you'd think I'd be used to whatever that woman might say."

"You're a saint, you know."

"No saint. I'm selfish. I keep hoping our kids are taking lessons and will take care of me when I'm old."

Tammy laughed.

"My mother-in-law is an incredibly strong woman and will probably outlive me."

As I left the store, I thought back to the very beginning.

"My mother wants to see you." Gary had ushered me to the back of the sanctuary. "Mom, this is Kathy. I'll drive the car to the front of the church."

Gary left me, a painfully shy fifteen-year-old scrawny brunette, standing with a woman a full head taller than me. Her shock of white curly hair framed her wrinkled face. Her austerity was intimidating.

"Well, since my son seems intent on seeing you, I guess we'd better be friends." She shoved her gloved hand toward me. "We'll be riding to church together from now on."

"Yes, ma'am."

"You are invited for Sunday dinner next week."

"Yes, ma'am."

The pastor and his wife stood at the front door when we walked down the stairs. I wondered if I looked as terrified as I felt.

Outside, Gary opened the passenger door and motioned us in. His mother scooted across the bench seat to the middle of the two-door Ford coupe.

The next Sunday when Gary arrived at my house, he whispered, "I'll open my door, and you slide in the middle."

I didn't look at his mother, but her stiffness told me she didn't like what had just happened.

My first meal in Gary's home was an old-fashioned Sunday dinner, consisting of pot roast, carrots, potatoes, and homemade noodles. Mrs. Crawford's apple pie not only looked perfect, but it tasted better than anything I'd ever eaten. I knew I'd never be able to cook like this woman. My shyness kept me from doing more than saying please and thank you when necessary.

Gary and I married two years later. We soon learned from a friend at church that Gary's mom had said, "Kathy isn't my choice for my son. I doubt they'll stay married six months."

Still married eight months later, Gary and I moved a hundred miles away.

I'd never called his mother anything, certainly never her first name, *Myrtle*. Now she was my mother-in-law, older than my grandmother. I couldn't call her *Mom*, *Mama*, or *Mother*. It didn't feel right. After the birth of our first child, my mother visited us for a few days and then Gary's mother arrived. That's when I started calling her *Grandma*.

Although Grandma had seven boys, my husband was her favorite son. Her sons all married, and it seemed to me that she loved "Little Ann" best of the daughters-in-law. She talked constantly about Ann's culinary skills, her perfection in house-keeping, and what a sweet wife and mother she made.

No matter what I did, I couldn't measure up. I learned to keep a neat house and to cook reasonably good meals, but I never received a compliment from Grandma. When she mentioned a perfume she liked, I bought it for her. Later I found she never opened it.

When she complained her purse had worn out, I bought her a new one. Two years later Grandma sent it to me, gift-wrapped for Christmas—a little used. When long skirts were popular, Grandma mentioned how much she liked them. I pulled out the sewing machine and made her a stylish skirt. She wore it twice and brought it back to me.

"Don't like it," she said, crushing my spirit.

When Grandma needed 24/7 care, none of her boys want-ed to put her in a nursing home, but none would take care of her either. Since Gary served as pastor and our 900-square-foot apartment was in the church, I had the perfect opportunity to say, "Forget it." Instead, I heard myself saying, "We'll manage somehow."

Neither Gary nor I realized how frightened Grandma might be on the main floor of a new home while we slept upstairs. The first night I heard her labored breathing, ran down the stairs, and called the EMT squad. Grandma was surprised I could hear her.

Many nights after that, I lay on one end of the sectional where she slept while she sat upright on the other. She seemed to enjoy our time together, talking about her childhood years and reminiscing about dogs her boys had owned. Tired, I found myself saying "uh-huh" instead of really hearing her, but still she always thanked me for being there.

With Grandma setting up her home in our living room, every parishioner who visited chatted with her. She always hauled out a beautiful tablecloth she'd crocheted in 1938, and we'd used at our wedding. "Took me a year to make this; Kathy wants it when I die because it's in her wedding pictures. If she's good enough to me, she'll get it."

Some guests thought Grandma was cute. I found the jibes painful.

Then on our twenty-fifth wedding anniversary, Grandma repeated what she'd alluded to when we married: "Never thought you'd stick around this long."

A few days later, one of Gary's older brothers and his wife visited us from out of state. Afterward, I learned Grandma had sent the coveted tablecloth home with them with instructions to send it to another brother.

I bawled for hours, until Gary snuggled me into his shoulder and said, "What were you going to do with it anyway? You can't take it to heaven, and it's too full of holes to use."

"I just don't understand. I do this and that and whatever to make her like me."

"Don't *do*. Just be you, because she needs someone to care."

I got over my hurt feelings and did my best to love her. I watched *Wheel of Fortune* with her, took her to the card shop, and helped her thread needles so she could embroider each of her boys one more set of pillowcases.

Grandma finished those pillowcases on a Friday. On Monday Gary said, "Mom doesn't seem quite right today. See what you think."

I took her to the doctor. He asked her the usual questions,

then about her family and what she enjoyed doing. Grandma answered every question clearly.

Out of her hearing, he said to me, "She's doing well for ninety-three. I'd say she's probably had a slight stroke. She's fine for the moment, but the next one might be a bad one."

For two days none of the family could entice Grandma to eat. Finally on Thursday afternoon, I spent the last of our grocery money buying the fixings for her favorite meal—fresh green beans, fresh strawberries, and Kentucky Fried Chicken with biscuits and gravy. The whole family sat in her room with her and reminisced while she ate. She finished most of her food and then smiled at me and said, "Thank you. That was the best dinner you ever cooked."

Grandma thought herself quite funny, and I finally did too. She died the next morning.

That summer Gary and I drove across several states to spend time with his brothers. My sisters-in-law confessed their jealousy. "All we ever heard is how you cook, bake, and sew, and about all the gifts you bought her. She wrote letters about the time you stayed up nights with her, and took her shopping too. Grandma bragged on you all the time."

"You've gotta be kidding me!" I announced.

On that visit I learned a lot of the family history and how little I knew about my mother-in-law. Then I grieved. I didn't appreciate her until she was gone.

Because I needed acceptance, I gave my mother-in-law gifts and did things for her. I think above all else she wanted some-one—me or Gary or the grandchildren or anyone—to spend time with her.

Some might say I learned Grandma's love language too late.

Not that I ever think we'd have been best friends, but after her death I realized Grandma's favorite son, my husband, needed me to freely give her my time. Grandma taught me a lesson of love after all.

*Katherine's husband, Gary, gave her some wise words: "Instead of trying to do, just be you, because she needs someone to care."*

*We live in a "do" focused world. We think if we work hard enough and do all the right things, we'll earn someone's love. Sometimes we wear ourselves out trying to gain approval and trying to prove that we care. We're so busy "doing" for others that we don't have the time to just be with them, to get to know them as a person, and to enjoy their companionship.*

*So often, people don't want us bustling around like busy bees on their behalf. Instead, if they could be vulnerable and verbalize their feelings, they would admit that they'd much rather we just spend time with them.*

### THE 5 LOVE LANGUAGES IN ACTION

The fact that Katherine's mother-in-law "bragged on her all the time" to her other daughters-in-law indicated that she did appreciate all the things Katherine did for her. However, her love language was not *acts of service* or *receiving gifts*. My guess is that her love language was *quality time*. Katherine said: "She seemed to enjoy our time together, talking about her childhood years and reminiscing about dogs her boys had owned. Tired, I found myself saying 'uh-huh' instead of really hearing her, but still she always thanked me for being there." The "thanks" came when Katherine gave her quality time.

## LOVE IS A CHOICE

Do you have in-law problems? Do you feel unaccepted by your in-laws? Do you know the primary love language of your in-laws? Few things are more powerful in changing the climate of your relationship than discovering and speaking the primary love language of your in-laws. For practical ideas on discovering someone's love language, visit 5lovelanguages.com and click on the "Learn" tab.

# The Day My Husband Prayed I'd Die

*LAQUITA HAVENS*

I did not realize how much my husband loved me until he prayed I would die.

His love had always been there. But I don't know that I'd ever really trusted it. After all, I'd loved my mom, and she had a history of running away. When I was nine, she ran away a month before Christmas and did not come home till many months later. No one knew where she was or if she was even alive. My little sister had her first birthday, and still no Mom. We never knew if she would come back.

My mom married four times. Dad married five times. I was a daddy's girl, in between his marriages. That left me with little faith in marriage—or lasting relationships, for that matter.

I mostly lived with my mom, until she left me a "goodbye, happy birthday" note two weeks before I turned fifteen. With the note was my birthday present, a new set of luggage. She wrote, "Be gone before I get home from work."

I went to school crying all the way on a city bus. School was a safe place to hide and pretend this had not happened. But it had, and I had no place to go, so I called my girlfriend. Her mom let me move in with them.

I married the first man who asked me. I didn't know if I loved him. All I wanted in a husband was someone to love me. My husband, Bruce, wanted someone to love, so it worked for us.

Ours was a lopsided marriage. He always wanted to show his love. He would offer kisses and I would brush him away—especially in public. I could not let the neighbors see any display of affection. It would be embarrassing.

I was too busy for hugs or sweet words with Bruce. I was trying to be a super mom and gave my children all the attention. Birthdays and Christmases were always special events planned for months in advance. I had no time to pamper my husband. I figured he was a grown man and he could take care of himself. After all, we are only children for a short time, and I wanted my children to have the best childhood *I* could give them. To do this, my husband had to work long hours, and I never told him I appreciated it.

I was busy working outside the home and doing many other projects when I encountered a major roadblock: physical pain. I had rheumatoid arthritis. I soon learned that dealing with any chronic disease is a battle. People I knew started telling me their horror stories. Someone had a friend who died of the disease. Another friend told me how long her mother and her family suffered. My best friend researched rheumatoid arthritis and reluctantly told me there was no cure.

These conversations continued for months. No one gave me any hope. There was never any good news.

Because of the pain, I couldn't sleep. Your mind plays tricks on you when you go without sleep. As if the pain were not enough, no sleep made fighting back so much more difficult. Each day seemed to last forever.

As the disease progressed, I grieved my loss of simple daily functions. Things such as tying my shoes and brushing my teeth became struggles that I sometimes left undone. I could not lift my arms. I would squeeze the shampoo in the shower by pressing it against the windowsill with my elbow, then not be able to lift my arms to wash my hair. One day I had to walk down the street to find a neighbor to open my front door. I did not have the strength to turn the handle. Lifting the phone required major effort.

My husband took over all the household chores, even the laundry. I discovered that I no longer cared how many clothes he put in one load, whether he put towels with sweaters and dress pants. When you are in pain, those details suddenly aren't important.

I had to learn how to let go of control and release my desire to have everything perfect. I'd always felt the children had to be perfect so everyone would know I was a good mom. The house had to be perfect in case someone came by. And of course I thought these things could only happen if I did them. That was me—always trying to please everyone . . . except Bruce.

Gradually I found new respect for this partner of mine. I knew he loved me, but I was afraid to love him, and most of all I was afraid to show him I loved him. In some warped way, I was afraid that if I showed him too much love, he would not work as hard to show me that he loved me. I needed to know he loved me because I never thought anyone could.

Years before, I'd thought as long as I had supper on the table, his clothes washed, and a clean house, I was a good wife. I never thought he needed time with me. Then everything changed. The children did not need me like before, and they had no time for me in my illness. How could I expect them to neglect their families in order to look in on me? I'd taught them well that children come first.

I was wrong.

When they were young, my children did need love and attention, but so did my husband.

I started realizing who was there for me: God, and the husband He gave me.

I did not want to be dependent on Bruce. It wasn't fair. I had never been there for him emotionally as he was for me. He should not have to wait on me, yet he was there, helping every way he could, and loving me through my pain.

During this most difficult time, Bruce had started a new job, so it was hard for him to take time from his work. He had to move to the second shift, and that left me counting the hours till he came home.

When the children were still home, I used to wonder what it would be like to have the house all to myself. Now I found it was not much fun. Bruce could watch whatever he wanted on TV, flipping channels to his heart's content. I just wanted him nearby.

As I began to look at my husband with new eyes, I realized Bruce deserved someone who would serve him, someone who would love him the way he loved me.

*He is so good, so gentle, so loving, and so kind. He has all the fruits of the Spirit. He is wonderful,* I mused. Then I realized, *I love him.*

I could not believe it. After close to forty years of marriage, I fell in love with my husband.

Everything was different after that. I could not wait for him to come home. I told him I loved him all the time. It wasn't hard at all. I was no longer embarrassed if he kissed me in public. I looked forward to his kisses. We took neighborhood walks, holding hands. It felt good to want to be near him.

It was so much fun loving my husband, hearing his voice, seeing his smile, hearing him laugh. If only I were not such a burden, he really could do so much better.

The pain was bad, even severe at times. Watching my husband hurt for me was worse. That's when he prayed I would die.

I was in my green recliner. Bruce had brought me my pain pill. He watched me bend my head and cover my face in defeat. It was useless to even try to hold the glass of water or reach for the pill.

He got on his knees, grabbed my hand, and prayed, "Father, if it is your will, take Laquita home so she does not have to suffer."

His tears splashed on my arm as I felt his whole body shake.

*He does not love me*, I thought with surprise. Then, in my heart, I knew he was praying this because he *did* love me. He loved me enough to give me back to God if it was God's will.

He did not want me to die because I was a burden. He was suffering because I was suffering. He did not want me to suffer if God had a better plan. He had done everything he could— even prayed the prayer he did not want to pray.

I know how hard it was for him to pray that prayer. I never felt so loved in all my life. I never loved my husband as much as I did then.

God said no to Bruce's prayer. In time, my doctors found the medicine that has kept my illness under control. I can now function and serve my husband and let him serve me without feeling guilty.

Falling in love with my husband changed my life. It was a gift I was afraid to receive. Falling in love is a risk well worth taking. I am no longer in that bondage of fear. I am free to love.

*Sometimes, like Laquita, it's hard for us to believe that someone else really cares. It's hard for us to rest in the assurance that this love is true—especially if we feel we are not giving as well in return.*

*And when we don't trust a person's love for us, we tend not to love in return. We tend to hold back, afraid of giving. It's like having a beautiful swimming pool in your yard, but not enjoying it on a steaming summer day for fear that you might drown.*

*While none of us longs for challenges, at times it takes the fires of life's trials to help us realize that another person's love is as pure, strong, and reliable as gold.*

*When we're willing to trust another's love, we can take the risk to be authentic. As we step out and trust another, we can swim in the cool waters of love, enjoying the refreshment and pure fun.*

*Have you only been putting your foot in the pool? Let go and jump in. The water's fine!*

### THE 5 LOVE LANGUAGES IN ACTION

When a child experiences abandonment in childhood, it influences their ability to accept true love in adulthood. The fear of abandonment keeps them from emotionally giving themselves to another adult, even in marriage. Laquita was controlled by this fear for many years. The unconditional love of her husband finally broke through the wall of fear, and she was able to see his love and trust him. She called it "falling in love" because it was the first time she had experienced the euphoric feelings of being loved. Bruce had spoken all five love languages to her, while receiving little love in return. Such love is only possible with the help of God, who loved us when we, too, were unlovely.

### LOVE IS A CHOICE

Do you know someone who was deeply wounded in childhood? Do you identify with the pain that makes it difficult to trust the love of others? If you experienced abandonment or abuse as a child, may I urge you to seek the help of a Christian counselor? If you are married to someone who experienced such a childhood, may I encourage you to also seek such a counselor? We all are influenced by our childhood, but we need not be controlled by such negative experiences.

# The Battle of the Dishwasher

*SUSAN STANLEY*

Before getting married, my husband and I went through premarital counseling. We touched on many subjects that spark arguments between a husband and wife: money, family, beliefs, goals, physical intimacy, etc. But nothing in those counseling sessions could have prepared me for the primary cause of our worst battles the first few years of marriage.

We fought over how to load the dishwasher.

My husband was reared with definite rules on how a dishwasher should be loaded, and each rule had a practical reason behind it. Plastic almost never goes in the bottom rack, lest it become warped. Forks should only go with other forks in the silverware basket, knives with knives, teaspoons with teaspoons, and soup spoons with soup spoons. If you do this, unloading is a simple matter of grabbing a handful and putting them away at once without having to sort through utensils.

Other rules come into play, but these will give you the general idea.

I grew up with basic guidelines that followed common sense (load the forks and knives point down to avoid stabbing yourself when unloading), but in the face of all of my husband's pragmatic rules, I rebelled. Why should I have to do it *his* way? My family managed to have clean dishes for years without following all those rules!

As petty as it was, I would thwart his rules where possible, just to do it my way—and to get under his skin, I'm embarrassed to confess. I loaded the dishwasher the way *I* wanted— he said he was attracted to me for my independence, right? Then I fumed as he came along behind me and rearranged items according to his preferences.

As is so often the case in marriage, our fights about the dishwasher escalated into bigger issues. I would get self-righteous and declare that no future child of ours should feel her best was not good enough. How would a small family member feel when Daddy came along behind them and "corrected" how they loaded their dishes?

I was sure our children would feel crushed and never feel satisfied with anything they did. "We live under grace, not under the *law*!" I announced more than once, sure that even the Bible would agree with me.

My husband insisted that the rules he followed were not arbitrary; they were in place for good reasons. Did I *want* our plastic dishes to be warped? Would I reject an idea out of stubbornness, even if it was best? He felt pride was an issue I needed to deal with—especially if it meant I was rejecting the *right* way to do things!

Somehow about the second or third year of marriage we agreed to live and let live. He would load dishes as he saw fit, and I would load them as I wanted. We agreed not to redo or "correct" the other's loading style, and we tried to extend more grace for each other—and have more humility.

He had a tough time overcoming decades of habit. I realized this the day I overheard him on a support call of sorts with one of his sisters. They coached each other about how it was okay, even if it was hard, to put teaspoons and soup spoons into the same divider in the silverware basket.

They had to talk each other into allowing a rule to be broken; it offended their natural inclinations! I think setting aside any loading rules must have been like hearing fingernails on a chalkboard for him.

I tried to recognize that what I considered small things actually required sacrifice on his part—and that he chose to make that sacrifice out of love for me.

Now I work to conform to his comfort level where possible, purely as a way of loving him. No, I see no need for all plastic to be in the upper rack, but does it cost me anything but pride to honor him in such a small way? He may appreciate my independence, but he appreciates it more when I choose to set aside my way to show my love for him instead of having to prove I'm right.

Early in our marriage we decided that aside from our individual relationship with God, no aspect of our selves, whether habits, choices, or personal preferences, was off-limits to change. I don't know if we made that decision by design or pure grace, but I suspect we stumbled into grace.

I don't want to hold any aspect of my life over my husband's head, saying it is more important to me than he is. If a choice I make pulls me away from a unified marriage rather than toward it, I need to recognize it and change. I am learning that marriage is more about surrendering than fighting to maintain self.

We still have our faults, and we are as different as we always were! It bothers me to this day that he does not anchor light pieces down in the dishwasher with heavier pieces so they will not flip over and fill with water during the wash cycle.

He still gets frustrated by the way I load glasses over the posts in a rack rather than between the upright posts. It still takes conscious self-control at times to prevent "fixing" how the other person has loaded dishes, so they are loaded as we each prefer them.

We had a rather amusing revisit to all our battles just a few years ago. My in-laws were in town and stayed with my parents. One of those days, my husband and I were in my parents' family room. From the kitchen, we overheard the same debates we had our first year of marriage: my dad had loaded the dishwasher, and my mother-in-law, loading her breakfast dishes, came along behind him and reloaded all the dishes the way they "should" have been loaded. She explained why she was changing things around.

My dad responded much as I had! Their debate ended much quicker since they were not married. We tried to stifle our laughter, understanding better why our battles had been so long and heated. We were also very thankful that we had reached a point that we *could* laugh rather than cringe!

We learned that a wholehearted relationship is not possible unless each person is committed to choosing love first. This doesn't just mean in the big areas of work, finances, family, and such, but also in the seemingly inconsequential things. We can ask, *Am I willing to set aside my pride for a very specific moment in time and choose to extend love and grace? In every confronta-*

tion, in every fight over whose way is right, will I choose love or will I choose pride?

With regard to choices, in baby steps over days, weeks, and months that gradually turn into years, we are learning to choose *us* rather than me—even in something so small, so petty, as loading the dishwasher.

*Have you ever found yourself in a heated battle with a friend or loved one about something that's actually rather silly? So many times we get all upset over differences of opinion or things that aren't important. But how these matters grow! Before long, our relationships are lying in a crumpled heap over which way the toilet paper should hang, or who treated whom the last time we went out for dinner together.*

*When little conflicts threaten to rip at the fabric of your relationship, one question to ask is: Does it really matter?*

*Is the issue we're arguing about more important than the relationship itself?*

*If we're holding on to our "right" to be right, we should just give in. If we're holding on to a silly argument out of pride, we should just give in. We don't lose when we graciously concede.*

*When it comes to fighting in a relationship, choose your battles wisely. Only use the emotional energy on things that really matter. And you might be surprised at how few things in life are really worth a fight.*

## THE 5 LOVE LANGUAGES IN ACTION

I can personally identify with this story. I am the organized one who thinks that everything has a proper place in the dishwasher. My wife loads the dishwasher like she was playing Frisbee. After many frustrated attempts on my part, she said to me: "If it is so important to you, then why don't you just load the dishwasher?" I agreed. So, I have been loading it for over forty years, and all is well.

It is always fine to request that your spouse change the things that bug you, but it is never right to demand that they change. If you are speaking their love language, they will likely be open to making changes. However, they will never do everything the way you prefer. Why? Because they are human. True love accepts the "imperfections" of others.

## LOVE IS A CHOICE

If you are married, what are the traits of your spouse that have irritated you? Now would you be willing to discover and speak your spouse's primary love language as a way of life? When you do so, you can begin to make a "request" for change from time to time. You may be surprised at their response. Don't expect perfection. If they choose not to change, don't allow irritations to divide you. Accept the reality that two people will never agree on everything. Love does not demand its own way but is open to changing things to make life better for your spouse.

# The Weather Kitten

*NANCY J. FARRIER*

I stared in wonder at the glass shelf filled with knickknacks. In my small town, the five-and-dime store was about the only place for a young girl to shop. The coins I'd saved bit into my palm through a cloth handkerchief.

*This is it!* I thought as my eyes landed on the perfect gift for my mother. I could almost see the delight on her face when she opened my present on her birthday. Excitement raced through me as I pointed to the small ceramic kitten so the storeowner could take it down.

The clerk handed me the off-white figurine, and I opened the printed tag tied around its neck. It read: The Weather Kitten. The rough surface of the small animal chafed against my hand as I read how the figure was intended to reflect the weather outside. On days when snow was expected, the kitten's coat would turn gray. Rain changed the finish to blue, and sunshine would be shown in pure white.

Each weather condition was listed with the color to look for, so you would know how to dress before you walked out the door. I smiled with delight as I paid the white-haired gentleman for my gift.

On my mother's birthday, I couldn't sit still as I waited for her to open my package. I knew that while Mother stood at the sink washing dishes or preparing meals, she often looked out the window and commented on the weather, surmising what we could expect if we went outside.

Mom loved to listen to the news to see what the weatherman would predict for the next day. I knew she'd be excited to have this kitten help her know what was ahead. I didn't stop to consider that she didn't care that much for cats. After all, I loved them enough for both of us, and this blue-eyed cutie was sure to charm.

When Mom pulled the kitten from the box, I edged forward, eager to show her all the ways this gift would be beneficial. We read the tag together, and she placed the ceramic cat on the windowsill where we could both check it each day to see what color the pebbled surface would show. Because it was December and we lived in a colder climate, I knew we would see more gray and blue than white.

Every day as Mom washed the dishes and I helped, I covertly glanced at the little figure. We had rain. We had snow. We had sunshine. Through it all, the kitten remained off-white, the same as when I'd first spotted it in the store. It refused to change color as promised on the tag.

Mom must have noticed my disappointment. I had saved my allowance to buy something special for her birthday. I felt like I had wasted that money. The kitten was cute but didn't foretell the weather. I wondered if Mom was also disappointed in me because I gave her a gift that didn't work.

"Why don't we move this to a higher shelf on the window," Mom said. "Perhaps the sill is too low for the change to occur.

The window frame might be blocking the light."

Day after day my mother would comment about the small cat. "Don't you think there's more blue in the coat today?" or "I'm sure this is a darker gray than yesterday. We must be getting ready to have snow."

I would glance outside at the low, heavy clouds and realize that even I could tell everyone it would snow.

Years passed. I grew up, married, and left home. Dad and Mom moved to a different house. When I visited their new home, I was amazed to see the small weather kitten on a shelf next to the kitchen window, still looking outside waiting for sun, snow, or rain. Touched that my mother would keep a useless gift, I began to ponder the lessons my mother taught me through the experience.

Mom didn't love that kitten, she loved me. She loved that I had spent my meager allowance to buy her something I thought she would like. Instead of being disgusted over a gift that was worthless, she saw the worth in the giver's intent. I have never forgotten that lesson, even though she instilled by example, not with words.

My mother also taught me to consider other people. I think of all the people in her life. She cares enough to learn small details about them, which she turns into little gestures of love that mean so much. Many times, she takes a piece of pie to someone in a nursing home because she remembers it is his favorite dessert. Mom makes homemade jams and recalls who likes which fruit so she can give them a jar. Because of her example, I've learned to listen to what others say about themselves. I know which people like certain foods or colors, and I try to incorporate that into a gift for them.

I learned that love is a matter of how you view life. When I looked at that knickknack, I saw failure and disappointment. When my mother looked at the same gift, she saw success because I'd chosen the kitten especially for her. To her, the figurine's failure to fulfill its purpose had no bearing on its value. The only difference between my mother and me was our outlook. Instead of viewing the negative, she saw the positive.

Mom showed me that love doesn't give up. We had many difficult years, times when I wasn't there for her or did things that hurt her. Yet she didn't throw away that kitten. She kept it in a prominent place, even though there must have been pain with the memories it evoked. She kept hoping our relationship would mend. When it did, she didn't flaunt her ability to love but continued loving as she always had.

Over the years, I've received my own share of gifts that were not what they were touted to be. I have several displayed in prominent places. Each time I look at them—especially my children's gifts—I think of the giver, and how that person thought of me when they chose that gift. I often recall a small kitten sitting on a windowsill far from me, and the final lesson: love teaches others how to love—and I have to smile. From mother to daughter to grandchild, a worthless weather kitten becomes the most precious gift of all.

*What a wonderful lesson for all of us: that love is a perspective. Sometimes people disappoint us by what they do or say. But what a great reminder to look beyond the outward appearances to the intent of the heart! When we focus on the heart, it's not hard to overlook another person's mistakes and failings. As one of the wise men of the Bible, Peter, pointed out, "Love covers a multitude of sins" (1 Peter 4:8).*

*And when we're the giver who's afraid we've disappointed someone we care about, let's remember not to underestimate the power of love. People who truly care do so because of who we are—not because of what we can do for them, or give to them, or be for them. Instead, those who love us see us with their hearts . . . hearts that look behind actuality to our motivations.*

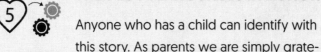

## THE 5 LOVE LANGUAGES IN ACTION

Anyone who has a child can identify with this story. As parents we are simply grateful that our child thought enough to buy us a gift. We see the child's heart more than we see the gift. Nancy's mom had learned an insight about giving gifts to another adult: get to know what they like, and choose a gift they will enjoy. When we give gifts, we need to consider this important insight. If we are on the receiving side, we also need to remember to see the person's heart as more important than the gift. Everyone is happy to receive a gift, but for some people, receiving a gift is their primary love language. When giving a gift to these people, we really need to take the time to learn the type of gifts they find most meaningful.

## LOVE IS A CHOICE

Have you ever given a gift and sensed that the person receiving it did not really appreciate it? How did that make you feel? Have you ever received a gift that was not meaningful to you? How did you respond? Were you able to see the heart of the giver, more than the value of the gift? Whether giving or receiving a gift, we can all learn from the example of Nancy's mother.

# Say Goodbye to Your Mistress

*JENNIFER DEVLIN*

"You know I love you, right?" he said with a sideways glance as he walked back into the apartment with a laundry basket full of warm, clean clothes. A smile crossed his lips as he studied my expression.

"Really? Wow."

Inside I was leaping with joy. But on the outside, these two simple words became my response to the pronouncement I'd been longing to hear for months. Maybe I was just stunned at the nonchalant way he stated his feelings. I'm sure my expression was comical—pure astonishment layered with complete relief.

We had met months earlier, at a workplace celebration just days before the Christmas holiday. He asked me out on a date. Dinner and a movie: safe, predictable, and surprisingly fun. We settled on a time for him to pick me up, and we parted ways, one rung above strangers on the relational ladder.

That next night we tromped through freshly fallen snow in the parking lot as we hurried into the warm hallways of the movie theater. When we settled into our seats, munching popcorn and waiting for the previews to roll, my man of few words pronounced a truth I wouldn't fully comprehend for years to come: "The army is my mistress."

*Yeah, right,* I thought. *What kind of comment is that? Why would he tell me that on a first date?*

I brushed it off but would have been wiser to heed the warning.

His reserved demeanor and polite banter were charming, but I didn't expect this to amount to a lasting relationship—unless he opened up a bit more. My aptitude for relationships was limited to what I heard and saw. I still had a lot to learn about love.

Months after that first date, when he carried his words of love with a laundry basket, our lifelong love affair finally began. Sure, we'd been getting to know each other, and yes, we liked to hang out together. But I believe true love begins when the secret longings of our heart spill out into our lives. His words connected with my soul. Until that moment, I'd been holding back my emotions. Now my heart was pressing on, full steam ahead, and ready to consider a life committed to this man.

We grew in our love, even though that looming mistress was always sneaking phone calls and nighttime visits. She (the army) was always calling. An urgent meeting here, a need to travel there, and he was off with very little explanation.

Insecurities plagued me as I wondered what he was thinking or how ready he was to share his life with me. I wasn't sure I wanted to share his attention with anyone—especially with what I considered a job instead of the *adventure* the television commercials described the army to be.

We continued to date. We toured the local sights and talked about our interests and general details of our lives. In the back of my mind I explored many hidden worries. *Can I love someone who seems to have such an emotional wall built between us? Will he ever openly express how he feels? Can I function in a relationship with someone so different from me? Will I have enough patience for long work hours and frequent separations?*

On our wedding day, I saw him standing there in his dress blues, and the reality of military life crashed in on me. It was true. The army was the 24/7 focus of a mind committed to protecting our freedom. Anything, even family, would have to take a backseat.

The love we shared only hit the number two slot on the top ten list of his life. I had to learn to share his love with duty, country, and freedom. Nothing would have kept me from falling in love with this man, and my sense of patriotism grew as I learned what compelled him to serve and experience the life of those who support our country.

While I wouldn't have changed a thing about his commitment to his country, I had to change my expectations. I was faced with the challenge of having to mature in how I handled relationships.

Through the next thirteen years of active military duty, our love weathered the storms of late-night office hours, deployments, training exercises, and community support. I learned to love through the times when he was half a world away, or when his dinner grew cold awaiting his arrival. I juggled the roles of being the dad, the mom, the nurse when our son was sick, and the playmate while Daddy was serving our country.

We experienced times apart with limited conversation before

the age of the internet and the cellphone. I was learning how to love beyond communication barriers in so many ways! Some years, this life's challenges brought such a feeling of distance in our home that I imagine we both prayed we'd find the strength to build intimacy in our marriage again. In the midst of deployments and hectic schedules, introverted men like mine tend to find little time to reinforce the walls of the home front through words.

We maneuvered through our relationship with the understanding that we loved and were loved—no matter the circumstances or trials we faced. I would survive every moment of insecurity and doubt if I recognized that his love was not limited to his ability to express it verbally. I'd be fine if I'd learn to love a man of few words.

What kept my love strong? My heart held on because of that simple afternoon affirmation. On countless days the image of my mate holding a basket in one hand and my heart in the other reminded me that we had a spark that had been fanned into flames. Underneath our daily lives was a love that would withstand any silence or separation.

Our relationship was built on trust, love, and yes, even a few words. Over time I learned to love beyond mere sight and sound.

My husband's expressions of love are found in a variety of ways—through integrity, honesty, service, and support. The more I understand how he shows devotion, the more I'm able to rest in the peace of knowing that I am loved.

At the end of twenty-four years, he said goodbye to his mistress. He retired, and in the blink of an eye, our family climbed to the top of his list. We were finally allowed to be the number one focus in his life, the prime target of love and priority. After years of figuring out how to survive as the shared love of a wonderful man's life, I was blessed with the realization that nothing could capture my husband's interest more than his family.

Our love still grows stronger. I wouldn't have traded a thing. I wouldn't have missed out on a second of military life. I wouldn't have wanted anyone else with whom to share my life.

But the in-between years have given me a glimpse into learning to love someone who approaches relationships far differently than I've ever experienced. After all, a man of few words is a complex challenge for any woman who wears her heart on her sleeve. And you know what? It's okay. I know he loves me.

*In an insecure world, it's not uncommon for us to want to have "proof" or reassurance that someone we care about returns our feelings of affection. Our imaginations interpret silence, distraction, and preoccupation as signs that the love is fading.*

*That's one of the reasons it's so important to understand the love language of a person we care about. Some people just show their affection in a different way than we do. And chances are, if we're in a friendship or a love relationship with a "strong, silent type," we're not going to hear or see frequent, obvious displays of affection.*

## THE 5 LOVE LANGUAGES IN ACTION

Jennifer's story illustrates the value of understanding each other's primary love language. My guess is that she and her husband were never exposed to the love language concept. She was longing for *words of affirmation.* This was not something that came naturally for her husband. He was not a "talker" by nature. However, had he understood the love language concept, he may well have learned to speak her language, and enhanced her security in his love.

To Jennifer's credit, she chose to look for the positive qualities of her husband and realize that these were expressions of his love. She gave him emotional credit for these qualities. When he brought in the baskets of cleanly laundered clothes, he was speaking *acts of service.* His devotion to serving his country also revealed this attitude of service. She chose to accept his "silent personality" and focus on his positive traits, which allowed them to have a positive relationship.

## LOVE IS A CHOICE

If you are married, what is your story? Were you exposed to the love language concept in the early years of your marriage? If not, did you feel loved by your spouse after you came down off the emotional high of the "in love" stage of marriage? Did you follow the example of Jennifer and look for the positive qualities of your spouse? Or, did emotional love fade? If you are still married, it is never too late to discover each other's love language, choose to speak it, and meet each other's emotional need for love.

Many divorced couples who have now read *The 5 Love Languages* have said: "If I had read that book when I was married, I think I would still be married." Wherever you are in life, understanding the love language of those with whom you are close will greatly enhance your relationships.

*The 5 Love Languages: Military Edition* deals with how to speak the love languages while deployed. I wrote this edition after interviewing military couples who had read the original book and discovered how to keep love alive even when they were separated by the miles.

# The 50/50 Proposition

*SANDY CATHCART*

As I looked at my husband, I suddenly realized this was it: our marriage had hit rock bottom.

Rock bottom came when the oldest of our five children was a teenager. We had recently lost our house to a fire, and with no insurance we found ourselves transplanted from our dream home in the forest to a crowded two-bedroom house in the middle of town. The crisis alone was enough to make or break a marriage, but the adjustment from country to city living nearly did us in.

When I opened my front door to holler for the children to come in for lunch, the echo resounded for blocks. I quickly learned that it takes less volume to yell down a city street than it does across twenty acres.

The children had their own problems. Coming from the country, they were tagged with names such as *goat ropers* and *hillbillies*. Our oldest son found a different way home from school every day to avoid the inevitable fistfight. Our youngest son dealt with the changes by turning into a whiner.

Yet through it all, my husband, Cat, faced the biggest adjustment. The company he worked for went out of business. He found himself in the unemployment line facing day after day of rejection.

If I had been wise, I would have helped him through that rejection, but instead I added to it.

I didn't feel Cat was reaching out to the kids enough. He didn't understand their problems. He didn't understand mine. How could I feed a family of seven with so little money? And we had no alone time. The boys had one bedroom, the girls the other, while Cat and I slept on a hide-a-bed in the living room. So, every argument—and there were plenty of them—involved the entire family.

On this particular day, my rock-bottom day, I resorted to tears while my husband stood over me and shared his views that our boys would have to fight their own battles. Cat's opinion came after I stepped between my oldest son and a neighborhood bully. "You have to stay out of the middle of it," Cat said.

I looked up at him ready to plead my case. Instead, I caught my breath at the shock of anger in his eyes. Where had the love gone? The concern? What had happened to the romance?

Some people talk about how in a moment of facing death their lives flash before them. That's what happened to me as I faced the death of our love. The long-ago months of courtship rolled before me like a newsreel running in my mind. When did Cat stop bringing me flowers? When was the last time he had taken me on a date? When was the last time he had invited me *anywhere*?

Suddenly, I had to get out. I ran through the door and jumped in my car, peeling rubber in the street. I could barely see through the tears. Without a plan, I drove. Who could I turn to? Who would understand? Cat was my best friend. If I couldn't turn to him—

That was the moment I realized I couldn't live without Cat and I couldn't live with him. *Ouch!*

I ended up on a dirt road overlooking the wild and scenic Rogue River. I planned to hurl myself into the raging water churning over Gold Ray Dam, but I lost my nerve. Determined not to let fear stop me the second time, I drove farther down the river, below the dam, and slammed the car to a stop.

I jumped out and started wading into the water. The Rogue River was famous for carrying people away. It claimed several victims every year. I figured I would just walk out until it carried me away, but this was not to be my day. I walked across the river, turned around, and came back.

It must have been the only section that was slow and wide enough to do so. Or perhaps it was God performing a miracle like He did with the Red Sea in the Old Testament. I returned to the car, wet and cold but still very much alive. Like others saved from the jaws of death, I sat there and bawled, pleading with God to help me.

I didn't hear an audible voice from heaven, but a slow awareness washed over me until I realized I had a lot to be thankful for. I had a husband who treated me with kindness most of the time. He was trustworthy and faithful, diligent in providing for our family, and a strong leader. Perhaps unrealistic expectations had been hiding the truth from me.

I returned home. Cat was out in the garage and didn't see me change into dry clothes. I never said a word about where I had been.

My biggest challenge stood before me. For the first time in our marriage, I had walked out on my husband. He was hurt and showed it by becoming a rock wall. My first tendency was to run away, head back to the river. Instead, I tried to touch Cat, but nothing softened. His muscles were hard and stiff.

I felt as if I had lost everything, but in truth, I still had something left to give, so I gave it: I prepared a simple meal for my family.

Sure, I felt like a workhorse. I wondered if preparing meals and cleaning house were all my husband wanted of me. If so, he could hire a housekeeper and a cook and do just fine.

Normally I would have gone on with such thoughts, but this time I decided to stop them. As I dished up mashed potatoes, I replaced my negative thoughts with good ones. These weren't just Pollyanna thoughts. They were true thoughts. My husband was kind. He was a hard worker. There was a time, though it seemed very long ago, that he liked to laugh and have fun. He taught the boys how to fish and ride bikes. He said the words "I love you" often. That alone was a treasure for which most women would pay money. He snored . . .

I dropped my fork and laughed.

My family all stopped eating and looked at me. I just shook my head. JayJay, our oldest son, relaxed and started telling a joke.

I wished I could share my joke, but I didn't think my family could quite understand. My husband snored when he slept at night. How funny was that? Most women would have to buy earplugs or something, but I slept best when Cat's snores filled the silence. Surely that was proof of our long-standing love.

I reached out and touched my husband's hand. This time, Cat's fingers folded around mine, and I saw the love in his eyes that had been there all along. I also saw the hurt that I had misread as hate. Was it my expectations of seeing my own needs met that had kept me from realizing the truth?

*Give more and take less. Expect less.*

The realization from the river of adjusting my expectations came back to me, and it is with me to this day. Like an answer to a prayer from a foxhole, it was God's answer to me. This insight not only colors the relationship between my husband and me, but it also colors all my other relationships. I've gained friendships that I would have been afraid to start, friendships where I receive very little in the way of someone calling or thinking of me, but friendships that have added depth and meaning to my life. Some people can never reach out for fear of rejection, but these same people accept love with delight and charm.

Expecting less, I am more thankful. Giving more, I receive more.

I have discovered romance—one that spurs storybooks and fairy tales—and I have found it in my own marriage. Cat is my shining knight, and I will forever be his beautiful princess no matter what time and age do to our bodies. Arguments are shorter lived than they used to be and come less often. I seldom complain about the raised toilet seat or even about the piece of plywood covering the dry rot of our kitchen floor. Toilet seats and kitchen floors come and go, but relationships last forever.

I've regretted words spoken in haste—pain caused needlessly when I've lashed out in hurt. Sometimes it's difficult to squash my expectations as I sit on the edge of the bed and wish my husband would come to me. But I have never once regretted laying down those expectations and giving more of myself by reaching out in love.

I've always heard that marriage is a 50/50 deal—each partner gives 50 percent and the other meets them halfway. Yet after nearly forty years of marriage to a man I can't get enough of, to a man I love more every day, I can say with resounding certainty that marriage is not a 50/50 deal. It takes 100 percent commitment from both partners.

This 100 percent commitment has brought me more and longer-lasting joy than any 50/50 deal could ever offer.

*One of the biggest fallacies about successful relationships is that they're a 50/50 proposition. As Sandy found, for the ideal marriage each person in a relationship has to give 100 percent. But in order for us to know peace and fulfillment we have to give that 100 percent, whether the other person is giving 100 or 10 percent. When we focus on where we have fallen short and work on that, we often see the other's percentage go up.*

*It's one of those paradoxes of life: The more we give of ourselves, the more we receive. The less we expect from others, the more we get.*

*Sometimes this doesn't seem fair, and it certainly doesn't seem to make sense. But it's one of the keys to a living, growing relationship. This is one of the great secrets for making a friendship and a love affair with our spouse work.*

## THE 5 LOVE LANGUAGES IN ACTION

Sandy demonstrated the power of unconditional love. It is easy to love someone who is loving you. But to love the unlovely is not natural. However, this is the kind of love demonstrated by God. The Scriptures say: "God demonstrates his own love for us in this: While we were still sinners, Christ died for us" (Romans 5:8 NIV). When I counsel someone who feels unloved by their spouse, I have often challenged them to a six-month experiment. I ask if they would be willing, with God's help, to speak their spouse's love language at least once a week for six months and see what happens. While I cannot guarantee a positive response from the spouse, I have seen many begin to reciprocate in less than six months. Love, spoken in the right language, stimulates love.

## LOVE IS A CHOICE

If you are married, ask yourself this question: On a scale of 0–10, how much love do I feel coming from my spouse? If your answer is in the 7–10 range, then you probably find it easy to love them. If, on the other hand, you are in the 0–5 range, it is likely more difficult for you to speak their love language. Would you be willing to accept the six-month experiment discussed above? Remember, love, spoken in the right language, stimulates love.

# For Richer or Poorer

*CHRIS WRIGHT*

The marriage vows were easy: "For better or for worse, for richer or poorer, in sickness and in health, to love and to cherish."

*For better or for worse?* That was no problem. We loved each other, and life could only get better once we were married.

*For richer or poorer?* Well, we knew we'd both be poorer for many years. We were buying a house, and to be honest, we couldn't afford it.

But *in sickness and in health?* When you're in your twenties, sickness means nothing more than the occasional cold or tummy bug. We could manage those. We'd coped with that sort of thing ever since we were born.

Then suddenly after thirty-seven years of a great marriage of loving and cherishing, Liz was diagnosed with Alzheimer's disease. And that really *is* a sickness.

No way was I going to let Liz go into a care facility. I could manage. And for three years I *did* manage. At first it was fairly easy. The medication worked, and Liz's memory score rose to the point where she believed she was better. But of course, nothing in life is that easy.

In August her memory became worse again, and she started to have behavioral problems. Hey, not to worry—we'd promised that we'd be there for each other in sickness and in health. I'd see it through to the end.

The changes were slow but steady. It was a bit like watching weeds grow in the backyard. Things happen so slowly you hardly notice—until you get back from a long vacation. That's when you realize how much the plants have changed.

But I didn't get that break, so I hardly noticed how badly Liz's condition was worsening.

Friends from church rallied round. They were great. A good friend warned me that I had to look after myself, but I was doing fine—apart from the chest and stomach pains that were nothing more than indigestion brought on by a little bit of stress. Not that the antacid did much good.

The local health authority sent a helper to give me a break during the day. As far as Liz was concerned, the woman was unwelcome. So was the next one, and the next. Liz thought they had moved in with us, and she was afraid to go to bed at night in case they were in the room with us. And I couldn't go out and leave Liz with one of the helpers anyway in case she became too agitated, so the stress continued. And so did the love. In fact, looking back, I can see that our love was actually strengthened.

The more Liz's condition worsened, the more my love for her grew. We'd always been a very loving couple, but this seemed like an extra special love, and she was able to return it with hugs and kisses. But it didn't solve the stomach pains.

One morning in March, I woke up with a crushing pain in my chest. It couldn't possibly be my heart, I reasoned, and anyway I had no pain in my left arm. Besides, I had to look after Liz.

Liz managed to get some antacid, and this seemed to fix things. The pain didn't return, and four days later I felt brave enough to look up the symptoms of a heart attack on the internet.

It seemed that a heart attack could start with stomach pains. Well, maybe it could, but I definitely hadn't had a heart attack. I knew that for sure.

Well, not quite for sure. On Monday morning I was seeing my doctor for a checkup, just to be on the safe side. He immediately transferred me to the local hospital for a checkup, also just to be on the safe side.

Liz had to go with me. I couldn't arrange for anyone to look after her until the afternoon, so she sat by my side, wandering off from time to time as she became bored.

The hospital staff knew she had Alzheimer's, but I was the patient and they wouldn't take responsibility for her. So, each time she went out of sight I had to get up to bring her back. I wasn't wired up yet, so it was easy enough.

Fortunately, my daughter was able to come from her work and take Liz home before lunch. A friend from church who had been a nurse checked on Liz during the afternoon. By then I was wired and tubed up and given blood tests. Yes, I'd had a heart attack.

"Will I be going home today?" I asked naïvely. "My wife needs me."

The family brought Liz to see me in the hospital the next day. Things were going well at home, or so they told me. They probably didn't want to add to my stress.

The tests showed that I had two blocked arteries that could probably be fixed with stents.

I had to stay in the hospital, and this could be a matter of weeks. I knew that Liz wouldn't understand what was going on, even if the family told her.

The next Sunday was Easter—the first Easter we'd not gone to church together. I was taken to the hospital chapel in a wheelchair, and after the service the chaplain asked me what was wrong.

I started to tell her about Liz, and the tears came. I couldn't speak. I'm sure the rest of those present thought I was crying because I'd been given the devastating diagnosis. Not that I cared what they thought. My tears were for Liz.

After ten days, the family was no longer able to cope. Liz had to go into temporary care. She had been brought to see me several times and knew I was no longer at home. Our oldest son bravely volunteered to take his mom to a specialist care unit, and I'm sure there were tears there as well.

The trauma of going into care was not as devastating for Liz as I had feared. She settled within forty-eight hours, and I phoned her a few times and said I'd be seeing her soon.

Nearly four weeks passed before I could leave the hospital, and this turned out to be a great blessing. Liz seemed to accept that we were parted, and the family could visit her without her crying when they left. The expert assessment on Liz was that she needed to stay in full-time care. So now I had to find a permanent care home for her.

The local health authority gave me a list of approved homes, and I quickly found one that seemed fine. I took some of her favorite pictures and ornaments to decorate her room in her new home and was in the room when she arrived.

Yes, there were tears, but there were hugs and kisses too. Liz never asked to come home. One day she asked me if we had a home somewhere, and I said, "No, not at the moment."

We didn't have a home. I lived in the house that had once been our home, determined to make the best of my life from then on.

Once Liz had settled in, I took her to the local church every Sunday. I didn't want to go to the church where we had first met and had worshiped ever since. I wanted Liz to think that she was living a new life, without remembering the past.

As Liz's condition worsened she had to be moved again, this time to a secure nursing home. The pictures and ornaments were there when she arrived. And so was I. She settled in again remarkably quickly and is still holding on.

In sickness and in health? Maybe deep down, all those years ago, I thought that one of us might get a serious illness later in life. But that was far in the future. I'm glad the prospect of long-term ill health never worried either of us, because when it happened, we had the strength to cope with it.

*For richer or poorer?* The house was eventually paid for, and things got easier financially for us as a family. But richer? Forget the money. Surely, the richness is the extra capacity we both discovered for love. The love was always there, but in the time of suffering it became greater and even more important.

I think back to our wedding in the little country church in the village where Liz was raised. We both said, "I do."

Knowing what I know now, would I say it again? Yes, I would, without a single doubt. We're both much richer for having said it.

*A wise mentor once said, "We often wish we knew God's plan for our lives. But we can be glad God doesn't lay out the direction of our whole lives for us to see—if He did, we'd probably run scared."*

*Likewise, it's probably good that when we begin a relationship, we never know where it will lead. If we knew ours would be one of those relationships, like Chris's, that would face pain and challenge, we would probably hesitate! And in doing so, we'd probably also miss out on some of the greatest joys in our lives.*

*While no relationship is guaranteed a pain-free future, as Chris learned, love is still worth it.*

*And how does love weather the storms of life? A firm foundation helps. One of the keys is to build strength and nurture love during the sunny, warm days of camaraderie . . . to focus on and deepen the closeness day by day. Then if the storms hit, we can survive them because our relationship is already firmly planted and rooted in deep soil.*

*Take time today to nurture your relationships.*

## THE 5 LOVE LANGUAGES IN ACTION

When we make our vows, we anticipate that our marriage will make life better, not worse—richer, not poorer—and will bring health, not sickness. Neither Chris nor Liz anticipated the Alzheimer's journey. Chris demonstrated his commitment by speaking the love language *acts of service* on the long and downward journey.

A few years ago, I coauthored a book entitled *Keeping Love Alive as Memories Fade: The 5 Love Languages and the Alzheimer's Journey*. I wrote it with Edward Shaw, MD, and his administrative assistant, Deborah Barr. Dr. Shaw's wife, Rebecca, was diagnosed with early-onset Alzheimer's disease. Dr. Shaw not only cared for her but discovered that the five love languages played a key role in how to effectively love patients with dementia. If you know of anyone whose spouse is suffering with dementia, I hope you will gift them with a copy of this helpful book.

Deborah Barr also wrote *Grace for the Unexpected Journey: A 60-Day Devotional for Alzheimer's and Other Dementia Caregivers*, published by Moody Publishers. I highly recommend it.

### LOVE IS A CHOICE

If you are married, what have you experienced that you did not expect? Reflect on the marriage vows: "For better or for worse, for richer or poorer, in sickness and in health, to love and to cherish." Ask yourself how well you have "loved and cherished" when things did not go as you expected. If you see some weaknesses in your behavior, would you be willing to apologize to your spouse for past failures? A better future often begins with an apology for past failures.

# Pulling Weeds on Blossom Trail

*CONNIE POMBO*

"Who's pulling out the wildflowers in our garden?" I asked.

"Oh, that must be Judy. She said our weeds were encroaching on her property," my husband replied with a grin.

"How would she like it if I traipsed across her backyard and cut down her trees that are hanging over our fence?" I retorted.

"C'mon, honey, Judy means well. She just likes to have things *her* way," my husband explained.

"But don't you think she should have called first to let us know that she was upset with our wildflower patch?" I asked.

Mark shrugged and finished reading the Sunday paper. He didn't seem concerned. After all, it wasn't the first time Judy had taken matters into her own hands when things weren't exactly perfect in the neighborhood.

We had recently moved into the development, which was a quiet community with a blend of working couples, young families, and retirees.

It was our oasis!

In fact, after twenty-seven moves in thirty-two years, we could finally call it home. Our townhouse was ideal. We bought the model home with a gorgeous view of the common property. We enjoyed an unobstructed view of spectacular sunsets from our patio, access to walking trails right at our doorstep, and friendly neighbors at every turn—except our next-door neighbor on Blossom Trail.

Since our townhouse was in the middle of the row of three, we were sensitive to making too much noise. But when a football game came on and my three guys watched the Giants face the Eagles, their shouts, groans, and roars rivaled any crowd in the bleachers. At those times, I knew Judy would call and tell us to turn down the volume.

It happened at the beginning of the third quarter after the Giants had scored a touchdown and the guys let out a "HOO-RAH!" Then—just as predictably, as the Philadelphia Eagles missed the interception—the phone rang.

"You answer it this time," my husband directed. "Tell Judy we'll turn the volume down."

I picked up the receiver and heard a familiar voice. "Hi, this is Judy. I wonder if you would mind lowering the volume on the television. It's a bit loud, don't you think?"

"I'm sorry, Judy, the guys are watching a football game. I'll tell them to turn it down a few notches. Thanks for calling," I added.

*Clunk!*

I waved the receiver in the air and said, "I guess she hung up."

Mark chuckled and said, "What were you expecting?"

It went on and on: a need to control our television, our yard, our weeds, our garbage cans, and the type of flowers we planted in the front yard. Not having a green thumb, I was just thankful that weeds prospered in our backyard—at least they added a little green to the dry patches on the lawn.

When Judy's daughter was born, I tried to take her something special—a pink rosebud outfit with matching socks and booties. Judy thanked me but mentioned that she already had something similar and asked for the receipt so she could exchange them!

Tears clouded my eyes as I rummaged through the garbage to find the sales receipt. While sifting through coffee grounds and orange peels, I thought, *What am I doing wrong? Even when I try to be nice, she still resists my efforts. That's it . . . no more!*

That evening, Mark put his arms around me and whispered, "It's not you, honey. Don't you realize that Judy has to be in control, and when she's not, she goes off on her tirades? You're not the problem. Just let her be!"

One year passed, then two . . . the same problems continued. One sunny afternoon in late April, I saw Judy take her daughter for a walk in the stroller and asked if I could join them.

"Oh sure," Judy replied. "C'mon, we're just going around the block."

I grabbed my sneakers and raced to catch up with them. As we walked, I listened. Judy was twenty-six years old and her parents had just moved away. She and her husband were having difficulties and Judy poured her heart out. I told her that she would be in my prayers, and if she needed anything, I would be available to listen.

Our walks became more frequent and so did the listening, which was difficult—at first—because I'm usually the talker. But the more I listened, the more I realized how much Judy needed to hear words of praise and affirmation. She was, in her own words, "always doing something wrong."

I came to realize what Judy needed more than anything else was unconditional love—not only from her family but from friends and neighbors as well.

When I asked if Judy had someone she could talk to on a regular basis, she mentioned that she and her husband, John, attended a small Bible study group. But often they couldn't go because it interfered with their daughter's sleep schedule.

*Aha! That was it . . . I can help,* I thought.

"No problem, I'll babysit Jennifer while you're at the Bible study. I think it's important for both of you; I would love to help you out," I offered.

The look of shock on Judy's face mingled with an expression of genuine thankfulness was the best gift of all. Tears filled her eyes. "I can't thank you enough. That is so kind of you!" she responded.

Every Wednesday I sat with Jennifer while Judy and John had a night out and some much-needed time together with other couples their own age.

In fact, I looked forward to Wednesday nights, caring for the "granddaughter" I never had. Weeks turned into months, and Judy was so overcome with my kindness she often thanked me with more tears of appreciation.

Judy's heart began to soften, as did mine. The comments about our front yard not being color-coordinated ceased. The trash cans didn't have to be lined up perfectly all the time. And the backyard weeds didn't automatically have to be cut back to coincide with Judy's planting schedule. Judy was becoming flexible in her attitude and more patient with us as neighbors. Progress had occurred in both of our lives.

A bond of friendship grew. Judy became the daughter I never

had. I loved spending time with her—frequently taking her to lunch and enjoying many afternoon walks together. My heart ached for this struggling young mom.

When my husband was hurt in an accident and came home from the hospital, Judy was ready with meals for breakfast, lunch, and dinner—not just once but three times. "I'm here to help," she whispered, while Mark slept on the sofa. "You let me know if you need anything."

"Thanks, Judy," I said. "You don't know how much that means to me." Her face beamed when I told her how much we enjoyed all of her meals—especially the baked blueberry oatmeal she brought over for breakfast that morning. Tears streamed down her cheeks. "No one has ever told me that I'm a good cook," she replied. I hugged her and said, "Not good—you're the best!"

Out of the former "weeds" from our garden have grown beautiful blossoms of love and friendship. It took time to cultivate those seeds, but today we are enjoying the fruits of our labor. We have forged a new road of neighborly love on Blossom Trail.

*When someone resists our attempts to show that we care, we can become pretty discouraged. But when Connie fell flat with her neighbor, her husband gave her wise words: "You're not the problem."*

*People who are tough to love are often tough to love for a reason! Sometimes, like Judy, they feel compelled to control their worlds. Sometimes they just don't know how to relate to other people. Sometimes they just don't understand what makes others tick.*

*When we realize we're not the problem in a relationship, it frees us. It lets us look beyond ourselves and keep trying to build a bridge without thinking we're the one who's doing something wrong.*

*When, like Connie, we keep reaching out in friendship, keep trying to break through, keep trying to understand and find niches of service . . . eventually we usually do break through to the hard-to-love person's heart.*

*And like Connie, we might even find a friend who becomes as near and dear to us as our own child. Persistence in love knits hearts together.*

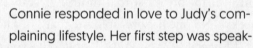

### THE 5 LOVE LANGUAGES IN ACTION

Connie responded in love to Judy's complaining lifestyle. Her first step was speaking the love language of quality time, as she and Judy walked together. Judy shared her story in response to Connie's willingness to ask questions and listen to Judy's heart. Then came the opportunity to speak acts of service in babysitting Judy's daughter, Jennifer, thus allowing Judy and her husband Mark to attend a couple's Bible study every Wednesday evening.

By this time, they were developing a genuine friendship. Judy's complaining stopped, and when she saw a need in Connie's life, she responded with cooking meals for her and Mark. When Connie responded with words of appreciation, Judy's response revealed that her primary love language is words of affirmation. "No one has ever told me that I'm a good cook." Connie's response was to reach out with physical touch as she hugged Judy and said, "Not good—you're the best." Connie's story demonstrates how unconditional love, expressed in the five love languages, can turn a complainer into a friend.

### LOVE IS A CHOICE

Is there someone in your life who regularly complains and criticizes you? Do you feel like nothing you do will ever please them? Can you see from Connie's story that most complainers are hungry for love? Their "love tank" is empty, and by nature they lash out at others, thus driving them away. It is the wise person who will take the first step in getting to know the complainer. As we listen to their heart, we look for opportunities to speak the love languages. Step by step we build a friendship, and eventually the complainer becomes a lover.

What first step might you take in getting to know the heart of the complainer? Would you ask God to give you wisdom and courage to take that first step? Who knows, you just might find a friend hiding behind a broken heart.

# About the Contributors

**GENA BRADFORD**—writer, speaker, and singer—has published in several anthologies, periodicals, and recordings. Her latest CD, *Given Wings*, can be found at her website: www .genabradford.com.

**LAURA L. BRADFORD** is a semiretired caregiver who enjoys encouraging others by telling stories about faith and family.

**STEVEN L. BROWN** is a cardiologist, clinical associate professor of medicine, speaker, and author of *Navigating the Medical Maze*. He lives with his wife and three children in Midland, Texas.

**SANDY CATHCART** is a freelance writer, photographer, and artist who thrives on a spirit of adventure and lives in southern Oregon. She and her husband, Cat, cook and guide for 4E Guide and Supply, a wilderness outfitter (www.sandycathcart.com).

**AMY CHANAN** lives in the Denver metro area with her husband and two children. She enjoys running, hiking, and spending time with her family. She is a member of Words for the Journey Christian Writers Guild.

**DORIS E. CLARK** is the mother of three and grandmother of eight. A member of Oregon Christian Writers, Doris has written devotions, articles, and stories for magazines and compilation books.

**KATHERINE J. CRAWFORD** and Gary, her husband of forty-nine years, reside in Omaha, Nebraska.

**BILLY CUCHENS** and his wife, Laurie, adopted their son when he was a toddler and adopted their daughter at birth. You can read Billy's articles on topics ranging from infertility to parenting on his blog, www.goggycoffee.blogspot.com.

**BETTY J. JOHNSON DALRYMPLE** lives in Parker, Colorado, where she spends time with Bob, and three children and ten grandchildren. When not enjoying traveling, she serves as liturgist for her church and facilitates a grief support group.

**MIDGE DESART** is a wife, mother, and grandmother. Besides being author of *Maintaining Balance in a Stress-Filled World*, she is a church musician and a beading embellishment artist. She and her husband live in Tacoma, Washington.

**JENNIFER DEVLIN** is the author of *Life Principles for Christ-Like Living* and the *Verses We Know by Heart* study series. Visit her website, www.ministryforlife.com, for more information about her speaking, writing, and ministry work around the world.

**PAMELA DOWD** has been a private school principal, preschool director, kindergarten teacher, legal secretary, children's clothing designer, freelance writer, and novelist. On street or treadmill, she enjoys reading and walking simultaneously!

**SHEILA FARMER** is a homemaker and freelance writer who lives near Annapolis, Maryland, where she is a columnist for the *Maryland Gazette.* She says, "I am ever inspired and blessed by my husband, Marvin Farmer Jr., and our two children, Shawn and Shannon."

**NANCY J. FARRIER** is the author of twelve books and numerous articles and short stories. She has five children and one grandson and lives in Southern California.

Having survived a flood, a tornado that snatched her house while she and her son were in the basement, and Hurricane Katrina, **REBECCA WILLMAN GERNON** believes if you can't find something to laugh about in every situation, you're taking life too seriously. She's currently waiting for a plague of locusts or a volcanic eruption to complete her disaster experiences.

**LAQUITA HAVENS** has been married to Bruce for forty-three years. A mom and grandmother, she loves to teach children through the art of storytelling and has written, directed, and produced puppet events for thirty years.

**CHRISTINE MCNAMARA** is a biblical counselor and teacher who enjoys developing resources to encourage and equip others. Her work includes a training manual for mentors to previously incarcerated men and women and a support group workbook.

**EMILY OSBURNE** teaches marriage workshops in the greater Atlanta area, focusing on engaged and young married couples. She wrote her first book, *Everyday Experts on Marriage*, in 2006.

**LAURIE A. PERKINS** lives with husband, Philip, in Needham, Massachusetts. A former children's librarian, she not only writes but also dances with the expressive worship team of Aldersgate Renewal Ministries.

**CONNIE POMBO** is an author, speaker, and founder of Women's Mentoring Ministries in Mount Joy, Pennsylvania. When not speaking or writing, Connie enjoys photography—one of her greatest passions (www.conniepombo.com).

**BARBARA L. SCOTT** (author of *From Rubble to Restoration*) and her husband are international ambassadors for YWAM. Barbara's passion is to use her writing and ministry to encourage others to experience God's ability to work all things together for good in their lives.

**NANCY PAGE SHEEK** lives in Columbus, Georgia, with her husband, three children, and three dogs. She enjoys writing, running, traveling, and hanging out with her family. Nancy has a passion to help set women free from perfectionism and performance.

**DONNA SMITH** is a retired classroom teacher who writes. Her works have appeared in *Guideposts*, *Sixth Serving of Chicken Soup for the Soul*, and *Bible Advocate*.

An escapee from the corporate world, **SUSAN STANLEY** is now a full-time wife to her husband, Trent, and mom to her two children. She writes during the children's nap times and at night.

**TAMARA VERMEER** lives in Colorado with her husband and three children. Besides writing stories and devotions, she is an avid reader who loves to reach women through Bible studies, writing, and just listening over coffee.

**FAITH WATERS** is an itinerant elder in the African Methodist Episcopal Church. With her MDiv in pastoral counseling, she has served as a chaplain at a youth detention center and as a youth consultant, and is a child behavioral therapist.

**CHRIS WRIGHT** was born in England, has written thirty books, and is senior editor for a small Christian publisher in Minnesota. He has three grown children.

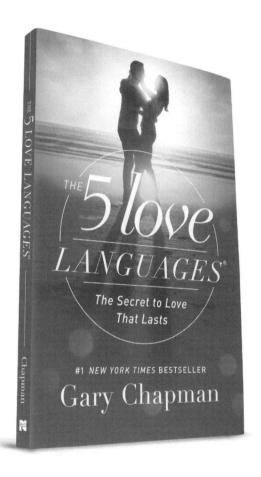

# GOD'S EXTRAORDINARY GRACE IS HARD TO GRASP—BUT MADE EASIER TO UNDERSTAND THROUGH STORIES OF GOD'S PEOPLE.

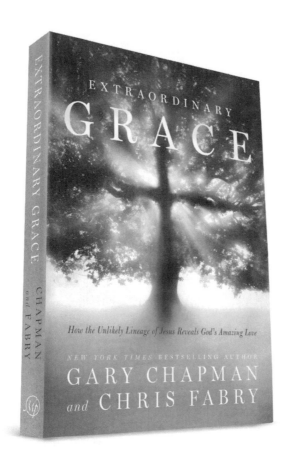

**MOODY Publishers®**

*From the Word to Life®*

Abraham lied. David killed. Rahab was a prostitute. What do all these have in common? They were broken branches on the family tree of Jesus. In *Extraordinary Grace, New York Times* bestselling author Dr. Gary Chapman and Chris Fabry dig into the amazing truth about the people God chooses to love. They're people frighteningly similar to you and me.

978-0-8024-1079-5z   |   also available in eBook